TARGETING DISCRETION

A Guide for Command Staff, Frontline Officers, and Students

Casey LaFrance, Ph.D.

With Contributions From:
Jonathan Day
Chad Ewing
David Rohall

UNG

UNIVERSITY *of*
NORTH GEORGIA
UNIVERSITY PRESS

Dahlonega, GA

Published by:
University of North Georgia Press
Dahlonega, Georgia

Printing Support by:
Lightning Source Inc.
La Vergne, Tennessee

Cover Photo:
Chevrolet Caprice Police Package. Black & White design. Titusville Police Department, Titusville Florida. Shot at the A. Max Brewer Memorial Bridge.
Photographer:
Gunner VV
Cover Photo License:
CC-BY 2.0

Book design by Corey Parson.

ISBN: 978-1-940771-09-0

Printed in the United States of America, 2016
For more information, please visit: http://ung.edu/university-press
Or e-mail: ungpress@ung.edu

Table of Contents

Acknowledgements

This work is the culmination of an incredibly intense few years. The support I've received and the hard work that others have done in the name of this project is simply amazing. I was very fortunate to have worked with a great editorial team, including editors April Loebick and Corey Parson, who guided me through the intricacies of the review process with grace and patience. I received helpful comments and suggestions from three anonymous reviewers, as well as the UNG Press editorial and faculty boards that left indelible impressions on the final product.

I am grateful for the many people who supported the research that led to the development of this project. My helpful and encouraging Department Chair and Dean, the graduate assistants with whom I had the privilege of working, my colleagues in the political science department, especially the political science department's Office Manager, Gail Ault, and countless members of the university community. Richard R. Johnson, Det. Stephen Johnson, Chief Israel Segers, Chief Chet Epperson, Chief Curt Barker, Brian Frederick, Vladimir Sergevnin, Stephen Taylor, Nikki and Ian MacKenzie, Matt Streb, Chris Bonneau, Julia Albarracin, Craig Tollini, Keith and Sara Boeckelman, Alice Sampson, Barry Friedman, Ross Alexander, Rosann Kent, Tad Scott, Chad Ewing, Jon Day, Erik Brooks, Kim and Tim Rice, Daniel Ogbaharya, Lona Panter, Kyle Rogers, Kurt Thurmaier, Roman Evstifeev and the Russian Academy of National Economy and Public Administration (RANEPA), Curtis Wood, Joe Medina, Josh Peters, Edward C. Peters, Sr., Edward C. Peters, Jr., Roberto Mazza, and Ben Green were instrumental in helping with various stages of the project. Many of these selfless individuals sat and listened as I tried to articulate various ideas in just the right way.

I am grateful for the police chiefs and sheriffs who opened their offices to me to allow for in-depth interviews and preliminary consultation. Moreover, I wish to thank those who responded to surveys I designed and administered with the enormous help of David Rohall and WIU's Western Survey Research Center. The National Association of Counties (NaCO) and WIU's Office of Sponsored Projects provided grant funding at various stages of my research career that allowed me to carry out this work.

Of course, I bear responsibility for any mistakes in the text.

More than anything, I am thankful for my family's support and sacrifice throughout this journey. My loving wife and best friend, Stephanie, listened to all of my concerns along the way and helped me to make sense of things. She paced the floors and chugged coffee with me through every phase of this project, but she also reminded me to have a little fun from time to time. One day, I hope to be the kind of person that she sees in me. Momma and Daddy showed unbridled enthusiasm for the project while my brothers, Cullen and Rodney, were willing to provide earnest feedback about the content and the aim of the project. While all of my aunts, uncles, and cousins also provided key support, Norma White's work in government and politics has been especially influential in my career choices and research interests. Garfield, Sylvester, and Tang always had an extra head-butt or purr when I felt overwhelmed, and my nephews and nieces made sure I always had time to smile. My faith in a just and merciful God has multiplied throughout the course of the project, and I lack the words to express how humble and appreciative I am for having the opportunity to do the job I love day in and day out. I have had the luxury of working with some of the best undergraduate and graduate students one could ever hope for, and I anxiously await the incoming classes!

I sincerely hope this book helps to stimulate discussions about decision-making in local government agencies. In some small way, I hope the tools contained herein are useful to the brave men and women who protect and serve their communities.

Macomb, IL
2/10/15

Introduction

Growing up in a law enforcement family, with a father and two brothers in the profession, ensured that dinner table conversation was never dull. Each night, there would be a series of tales from beyond the blue line. These stories ranged from guffaw-inducing to just plain strange. Some were downright shocking, and some were just sad. Trying to best one another, my father and brothers would take turns telling the exploits of their respective co-workers. Once they told of a time when a tiny senior citizen attempted to smuggle a twenty pound ham under her skirt at the grocery store. Another story was of when police found a lady calmly eating soup, beans, and cornbread at the scene in the aftermath of killing her husband with a series of blows to the head with a cast iron skillet (after being stabbed by the husband, no less)—her only request was to finish her meal before being taken off to jail.

These stories inspired such curiosity that I decided to give the law enforcement career a whirl. In this capacity, I was not disappointed in witnessing stories of my own. My familial background and work experiences raised my curiosity regarding the use of discretion as a backdrop to law enforcement accountability. I decided to devote a great deal of my research agenda to this phenomenon. This book is a result of this decision and will explore several questions piqued by my curiosity and observations. Throughout each chapter, I will operationalize discretion as follows: discretion is a product of the specialized, professional decisions and actions that a public administrator makes or takes in order to manage expectations (demonstrate accountability), fulfill duties (satisfy job responsibilities), and affect what he or she believes is the best possible outcome in a specific situation. While the use of discretion is necessary in every professional field, this necessity is especially palpable in law enforcement due to the autonomous nature of the job, the constant pressure officers face to make decisions and take actions quickly, and the quite literal life or death consequences that may result from these decisions and actions.

As with other books on discretion, this one may seem, at first blush, to be overly ambitious. How, the reader may rightly ask, can such a complex topic be treated adequately in an academic work? Moreover, how can scholars relate and empathize with the nit and grit of daily decision-making behind the badge? With these questions in mind, some caution may go a long way. The work that follows is not meant to be considered a cure-all for the nuances and dilemmas an officer or command staff member (anyone above the rank of patrol officer) may encounter by the nature of his or her job to make discretionary choices. Instead, this work is intended to provide these officers and managers a common vocabulary that may be used to build trust and mutual understanding at an interpersonal level, one-on-one, and throughout the organization. The Target Model of Discretion is a unique theoretical framework, based on a literal target upon which managers and subordinates visualize priorities related to the use of discretion. While the Target Model of Discretion may be used as a first step toward planning, goal-setting, etc., its most immediate use is in revealing points of divergence between rank levels and helping with organization development efforts to discuss and, sometimes, reconcile these differences. In sum, the Target Model presented is a tool for any given police organization to aid communication, especially between managers and subordinates.

The topic of police discretion has long intrigued members of the academic community and law enforcement practitioners. To provide a sense of the ubiquity with which this term has been studied, a Google Scholar search for "police discretion" yields nearly 10,900 results. A cursory scan of professional association publications such as *Police Chief Magazine* reveals a bevy of articles on this topic. While much has been written on the topic, the academic and professional literatures have left a glaring gap in their work: they have not conceptualized the multiple influences on discretion as operating independently of one another and with disparate importance.

This book is an attempt to create conversations between the academic community and law enforcement practitioners in order to advance our collective understanding of the factors that contribute to discretionary decision-making. The model presented in the pages that follow is designed to link theory and practice in a practical manner that should be implemented with regularity. To help scholars and practitioners, the model's research is intended to help these groups identify and categorize various observed types of discretionary decision-making. This theoretical framework allows for real-time comparisons of the determinants of discretion and opens avenues for exploring the roots of differences, especially between rank levels. Beyond this, the model makes an explicit yet simple and intuitive moral claim: managers and subordinates should communicate with each other about sources of discretion and their relative influence. I do not intend to suggest that managers and subordinates (or academics) should all have the same priority rankings when it comes to these sources of influence; one's relative position in an agency and his or her experiences might serve to illustrate the need for differences.

The model's basic premise and its research establishes that law enforcement practitioners (both managers and subordinates) and academics should be able to engage in constructive conversations bent on fostering empathy and understanding about the ways in which discretion is exercised. The latter group, academic scholars, provide a vital linkage between theory and practice. They train public administrators and provide crucial information regarding program design, policy implementation, and public opinion. Too often, a mutual skepticism develops between practicing police workers and scholars. Practitioners have been known to accuse academics of developing theoretical devices that have minimal utility in its real-world application. Academics may be disappointed that practitioners are unaware of empirical discoveries which have the potential to improve agency performance. Demonstrating the potential for a symbiotic relationship between these two groups is the first step in leveraging the value that each may add to the other.

To aid readers and to direct them to parts of this book that might be particularly appealing, I will briefly explain the book's layout. The book is divided into three sections. Part I consists of Chapters One and Two. Chapter One provides a survey of the discretion literature serving two broad purposes. First shown are specific factors important for the development and use of discretion cited in the literature. Afterward is a discussion on how the literature has yet to provide a means by which scholars and practitioners can offer attention to each of these sources simultaneously while also assessing the relative degree of influence they carry.

Next, Chapter Two shows how, in the course of interview research comparing accountability considerations between sheriffs and police chiefs, the Target Model development captures response differences offered by each type of manager. Part I's agenda establishes the foundation which the Target Model's research has been built upon.

Afterwards, Part II, beginning with Chapter Three, showcases the results of three case studies from my consultation with police agencies in the Midwest and South, exhibiting the Target Model's viability in constructing single case study research pieces. Here, the Target Model also provides practitioners preliminary diagnosis and guidance. Next, demonstrating the theoretical and empirical utility of the Target Model, Chapter Four focuses on the Target Model's use as a survey research tool for aggregate studies involving a large number of agencies. Aided by this preparation, we then can look at the nuts and bolts of applying the model in a real-world organizational setting.

Part III is intended to be the most practical, hands-on portion of the book. Here, readers will find several tools they may use to initiate and provoke discussions of discretion. Part III begins with a short chapter (Chapter Five) which lays out the hands-on process of using the Target Model for asking questions about the sources of discretionary choices, especially between rank levels in a law enforcement agency. An ambitious law enforcement manager can quickly read through this chapter and immediately develop a plan for diagnosing communication about discretion in his or her agency. Similarly, a scholar who wishes to replicate studies using the Target Model can easily design a research project using this simple step-by-step guide.

Subsequently provided in Chapter Six is a basic glossary-style overview of each of the factors cited as influential in discretionary decision-making. Afterward, readers will find a set of reflection questions for each category that may be completed in individual or group settings. Following the questions, readers will then encounter some fictitious scenarios that highlight one category of influence. These scenarios, too, are relevant for individual and/or group training.

The summation of these three parts displays the versatility and flexibility of the Target Model as a diagnostic tool, a training aid, and a theoretical device.

The book's conclusion addresses potential criticisms of the model and discusses some of the model's limitations as a diagnostic device. The conclusion offers readers some ideas about how, with future research and training, the Target Model can be improved and built upon. Preceding the concluding chapter, a practitioner-oriented guide is included for strategic planning that may be used after collecting agency-wide data using the Target Model.

Before beginning, a note of caution is appropriate. Because this text is intended for practical and classroom application, it attempts to strike a balance between these two very different worlds. This is, in many respects, a fundamental challenge in all public administration scholarship. Perhaps more candidly, this book is not designed for use as a stand-alone course text. Instead, the book will serve as a useful supplement to criminal justice, organization theory, and public administration courses while also retaining its utility in training contexts. While it is true that a wider theoretical net could have been cast, this book is exciting because it demonstrates how the convergence of theoretical frameworks regarding discretion can elicit an intuitive, easily wielded toolkit for students and public managers.

Part I

Chapter 1

The Evolution of Research on Discretion and the Need for the Target Model

Student Learning Outcomes	Practical Learning Outcomes
Students will appreciate the historical trajectory of research on discretion.	Practitioners will see how scholarship related to their work has helped bridge the gap between academia and police work.
Students will understand the need for a more nuanced and more holistic model of discretionary decision-making.	Practitioners will be able to relate their past and future experiences with discretion to the Target Model.
Students and Practitioners will become familiar with the vocabulary used in describing the Target Model guide.	

The exercise of discretion by frontline police officers is a commonly cited yet rarely understood phenomenon (Mastrofski, 2004). Scholarship has shown that police officers use discretion in order to: (1) reduce the complexities of their task environment and (2) identify concrete priorities that appear more personally meaningful than the vague, abstract, and often contradictory goals set forth by policymakers and managers (Lipsky, 1980; Maynard-Moody, Musheno, and Palumbo, 1990).

Oberweis and Musheno (1999) argue that a police officer's discretionary behavior is the product of a two-stage process. First, an officer uses mental shortcuts to define those with whom he or she interacts in relation to his or her own identity, defined as the sum of the officer's "multiple and intersecting subject positions," or ever-present roles and group memberships (Oberweis & Musheno, 1999, p. 899).

After developing these mental shortcuts, the officer is able to create mental representations for different types of individuals and apply these to his or her personal moral principles in order to decide upon what he or she believes to be a proper course of action in a given situation. Because every officer has a unique collection of subject positions, the common subject position of police officer is a faulty predictor of an officer's discretionary behavior. That is, even though they share an occupation, their life experiences and demographic characteristics may be sufficiently different to result in discretionary behavior that is not predictable solely based on knowing their occupation.

For instance, Oberwise and Musheno explain that officers whose identity includes certain subject positions (LGBT, minority, female, etc.) may define citizens who share these subject positions in starkly different ways than those officers who do not occupy these subject positions (e.g., heterosexual, Caucasian, male, etc.), leading to different outcomes in police interventions between a given officer and a citizen. These behaviors are characteristic of what Maynard-Moody and Musheno (2003) call a "citizen-agent" model, which the authors argue may complement understandings of frontline discretion derived from the traditional "state-agent" model. The state-agent model centers on how frontline bureaucrats "apply the state's laws, rules, and procedures to the cases they handle." In contrast, the citizen-agent model "concentrates on the judgments that frontline workers make about the identities and moral character of the people encountered and the workers' assessment of how these people react during encounters" (Maynard-Moody & Musheno, 2003, p. 9). In differentiating these two models, the authors explain, "The state-agent narrative is about law abidance, both of citizens and workers; the citizen-agent narrative is about normative or cultural abidance, identifying those who are worthy citizens and colleagues and those who are not" (Ibid, 2003, p. 9).

If identity-based personal morality (the citizen-agent model) is the basis for the officer's choice of action rather than written law (the state-agent model), officers cannot be expected to learn appropriate discretion using the same broad training mechanisms as those used to teach about the law. Throughout his or her pre-employment life, an officer accumulates values, attitudes, and cognitions that are never formally taught and might contrast with agency instruction. These facts may help explain why, to the chagrin of some social scientists, police discretion has come to be seen as a craft rather than a science (Mastrofski, 2004). Still, despite the variety and stability of personal beliefs, values, and prejudices, there are some powerful outside forces that work to shape officer discretion, and these lend themselves to systematic analysis.

COMMUNITY NORMS

The first of these forces is found in the collective norms of the community in which the agency operates. In essence, these collective norms are agreed upon expectations for what constitutes acceptable behavior. Here, a practice becomes a norm for one of two reasons: "the practice is believed to have inherent value," or "the practice is believed instrumental to accomplishing something that has value" to the community (Mastrofski, 2004). Attention to community norms has become increasingly common in law enforcement management since Wilson's famous "broken windows" thesis was presented (Wilson & Kelling, 1982; LaFrance & Lee, 2010; Russell, 2013; Kappeler & Gaines, 2012). Public intellectual and academic powerhouse, James Q. Wilson, suggested that changing the norms within a community for dealing with minor issues, such as broken windows or graffiti, would result in lower crime rates of this and more serious varieties.

FORMAL TRAINING

Another mechanism that shapes discretion is formal training concerning specific situation types (e.g., hostage negotiation). As mentioned above, broad training cannot account for every situation that officers encounter. Furthermore, some values and attitudes are so deeply ingrained in the mind of a new officer that no amount of training will change them. Despite the limitations, training does have a role in orienting a new officer to specific boundaries of discretion in certain situations (Gaines & Ricks, 1978). In fact, some scholars argue that appropriate discretionary boundaries are "hazy" because law enforcement managers fail to "take the initiative in carefully identifying the goals (and order of priority among them) that should be served during police actions," and these managers fail to "specify with any precision the best means of accomplishing these goals" (Fyfe, 1996, p. 184). Thus, Fyfe (1996, p. 199) argues, law enforcement managers who have "taken the lead in formulation and enforcement of policy to define and limit line officers' discretion" have been very successful. Continual training sessions beyond the initial academy experience provide the opportunities necessary for chiefs and sheriffs to clarify their goals and inform officers of discretionary imperatives and boundaries in certain situations. Thus, while no amount of training will be able to account for every situation an officer faces, training centered on specific issues (domestic violence, hostage negotiation, racial profiling, etc.) can be helpful to new officers. More importantly, such training can limit the police organization's legal liability in the event that a court decides that an officer's discretionary behavior was out of bounds (Clarke & Armstrong, 2012; Lee & Vaughn, 2010).

External Systemic Actors

A third source of influence on officer discretion is found in external criminal justice system actors. Nillsson (1972/1978) suggests that just as all law enforcement organizations have a unique informal culture, they also have a series of relationships with other actors in the criminal justice system (e.g., judges, prosecutors, etc.), and cues from these actors can influence officer discretion. For instance, a prosecutor's reluctance to try sexting offenses might curtail an officer's motivation to arrest or cite offenders for sexting (Walsh, Wolak, & Finkelhor, 2013).

Peer Influence, Mentorship, and the Informal Organization

Another force that helps to shape discretion surfaces is the informal organization. The informal organization is the system of expectations among workers that develops separately from codified organizational rules or standards. Management scholars have long considered the informal organization as a source of cues about unwritten agency policies and norms (Barnard, 1938; Roethlisberger & Dickson, 1929; Mayo, 1933). In local law enforcement, an officer learns the imperatives of the informal organization through peer interaction and mentorship between officers (Maynard-Moody & Musheno, 2003). Matrofski (2004, p. 104) contends that this leads to a "punitive bureaucracy" that curtails undesirable behavior but does little to "promote desired [behaviors]." Furthermore, the influence of the informal organization leads Bordua and Reiss to write that "internal solidarities create special barriers to the effective exercise of command over and above the features of task organization . . . the police commander ignores this internal culture at his peril. It can confront him with an opposition united from top to bottom" (1966/1978, p. 218).

Thus, Mastrofski (2004, pp. 104-105) contends that the "police culture" should be "assessed as an independent influence on the exercise of discretion." Because each agency has an informal organization based on peer cohesion (More, Wegener, Vito, & Walsh, 2006) and the need for acceptance, it is a common source of discretionary influence (Reiser, 1974/1978). Law enforcement officers must be attuned to this informal organization in order to survive (Reiner, 2010; Crank, 2010; Sampson, 2011).

EXPERIENCE

A final determinant of officer discretion is an officer's experience. Despite each new officer's unique composite of subject positions and values, it is common for new officers to perceive situations only in black and white and to vigorously enforce the law. This has come to be called the "John Wayne Syndrome" (Reiser, 1974/1978). As Reiser explains,

> [T]he symptoms of this malady are cynicism, over-seriousness, emotional withdrawal and coldness, authoritarian attitudes, and the development of tunnel vision . . . [leading to a perception that] there are only good guys and bad guys and situations and values become dichotomized into all or nothing. (1974/1978, p. 244)

This "syndrome," Reiser notes, is essentially a defense mechanism used to "protect the young officer against his own emotions as well as outside danger while he is maturing and being welded by experience" (1974/1978, p. 244). In previous research that I conducted, a sheriff used an analogy to explain why new employees have minimal value to his agency during this phase (in this instance, he replaced "John Wayne" with "Wyatt Earp," but the reader will note that the sentiment is similar to what Reiser describes). This sheriff spoke in terms of imaginary "degrees" that his staff earned after serving for specific periods of time, saying,

> You're not worth much to us when we hire you until you get five years on the street. Then, we think you've got your BA degree. You don't have your master's or PhD yet. But, at five years, we ought to know who you are and . . . that you understand how to do your job and treat people and how you fit into the system. . . .You ought to understand more about the subject matter you're dealing with. You've already worked through the Wyatt Earp syndrome, the

black and white syndrome, the no grey syndrome . . . and you've done those things that people normally do, but at five years, you're of some value to us.

Fortunately, the John Wayne syndrome only lasts for the first three to four years, according to Reiser, or five years, according to this sheriff. Once officers have passed this stage, they are more capable of seeing grey areas within the law, and are said to be "functioning as a professional" (Reiser, 1974/1978, pp. 244-245).

Because new officers in both sheriffs' offices and municipal police departments are vulnerable to the lessons garnered from experience, I expect managers will agree upon the role of experience in cultivating officer discretion (LaFrance & Day, 2013; Tillyer & Klahm, 2011).

An Agency's Need for Standard Operating Procedures

In describing the typical characteristics of bureaucracies, Weber explains that "[t]he management of the office follows general rules, which are more or less exhaustive, and which can be learned" (1946, p. 50). These general rules, often called standard operating procedures (SOPs), are necessary because they serve to mitigate organizational complexity and coordinate work toward common organizational missions or goals (Gulick, 1937; Romzek & Dubnick, 1987). Thus, in the view of early management scholars such as Frederick Taylor, individual talent is worthless "unless every man on the team obeys the signals or orders of the coach and obeys them at once when the coach gives those orders" (Taylor, 1911).

In addition to coordinating effort effectively to ensure efficiency, standard operating procedures serve to limit an agency's perceived legal liability because case law changes are incorporated into the SOPs (Romzek & Dubnik, 1987). This consideration is especially pertinent to the local law enforcement manager because agents are granted the power and authority to suspend an individual's freedom, to search and seize property, and to use various levels of force, including deadly force, to gain compliance from the public. With this in mind, local law enforcement managers must keep a keen eye on case law and court rulings throughout the nation, and consistently revise their policy manuals to remain compliant (Caplan, 1967; Ward, 2002; Ashworth, & Horder, 2013; Skolnick, 2011).

Thus, I expect that law enforcement agencies proactively craft SOPs for two complementary reasons: to articulate expectations in order to coordinate effort toward a common organizational end (what behavioral psychologist B.F. Skinner calls a positive reward perspective), and to avoid legal sanctions (what Skinner calls a negative reward perspective) (Skinner, 1957).

Whether a given policy is written out of a desire to earn a reward or to avoid punishment, it is impossible for even the most comprehensive policy to account for the unique nature of some of the situations a patrol officer or deputy sheriff might encounter. As one sheriff explained in an interview,

> What's the most complicated job in the world? I'll submit that it's being a police officer or deputy sheriff, and I'll tell you why. It's not because we have to be rocket scientists. It's because our subject matter is human beings, and they are the most complicated things we know with all kinds of variance capabilities within their reaction[s].

Beyond the limitations of a given policy, there is another reason that public managers may be leery of overemphasizing the importance of the SOP. As Merton (1940) argues, too great an emphasis on agency rules can lead bureaucrats to displace the actual goals of the organization and make following these rules their goal. Following the rules for the sake of following the rules, Merton continues, can hamper an employee's ability to think creatively or even think as an individual. This line of thought led one sheriff to conclude, "I'd rather have a band of rogue pirates out there investigating crimes than a bunch of officers who are afraid to do anything because they might be caught outside of the operating parameters of the policy and procedure manual." Statements to this effect suggest that there is more to an officer's job than simply complying with an agency's policy manual; these statements highlight the need for some degree of professional autonomy, allowing the officer to make discretionary decisions based on the officer's particular expertise (Davis, 1996).

An Officer's Need for Professional Discretion

Why do few people visit an auto mechanic for diagnosis or a doctor for medication when they fall victim to influenza? Why are there so few calls placed to the parks and recreation department when a building catches fire? These illustrative questions are easily answered in the context of professional expertise. These questions remind the reader that we often take for granted that someone wearing a police officer's uniform is expected to perform specific duties based on specialized training. Thus, residents expect a police officer to demonstrate competence, familiarity with a variety of situations, and a unique capacity for problem-solving, which are all dimensions of what social and organizational psychologists John French and Bert Raven (1959) call "expert power."

As discussed above, however, law enforcement officers are also expected to follow agency rules and regulations, most of which are written so broadly that they fail to give step-by-step instruction for the officer's behavior in a given situation (Lowi, 1969). Furthermore, in moments of crisis, these officers are often forced to make split-second decisions with potentially life-altering consequences with no time to flip through the policy manual. In less adventurous circumstances, officers may find that the policy manual is too restrictive to allow them to perform their professional duties (Lipsky, 1980; Maynard-Moody & Musheno, 2003), and that broad agency rules fail to account for the interpersonal dynamics inherent in the service provider's relationship with a client (Harmon, 1981).

In instances such as these, the previously described rationale behind creating and implementing a collection of standard operating procedures may come in conflict with the autonomy a professional officer expects to be afforded. Even more troubling, according to many respondents, is that the proper application of discretion only comes with experience. Thus, officers cannot competently exercise this important tool immediately upon graduating from a police academy. On-the-job experience is crucial to the development of discretion because it allows an officer to appreciate the grey areas of law enforcement (Reiser, 1974/1978), and as one sheriff explained, "You can't read it in a book or buy it at the drug store. You have to learn it through experience."

The Roots of Discretion

To summarize, the roots or determinants of discretion for any given officer are numerous. An officer's collection of "subject positions" and personal values influence discretion by helping the officer differentiate between those believed to be "good guys" and those viewed as "bad guys" (Maynard-Mooney & Musheno, 2003; Oberweis & Musheno,1999). External systemic actors (Nillsson, 1972/1978), community norms (Mastrofski, 2004), and lessons learned via formal training (Fyfe, 1996; Gaines & Ricks, 1978) are notable influences on discretion. While all of these factors are present in the development of officer discretion, the influence that each exerts varies with the law enforcement context in which these factors operate.

Defining the Boundaries of Proper Discretion

The primary difficulty in studies of discretion is ascribing relative weights to each source of influence. A frequently visited starting point for such discussions comes from legal scholar Ronald Dworkin's (1977) "doughnut model" of discretion. In the doughnut model, the doughnut hole is the sphere of appropriate discretion an officer may use. The doughnut ring serves as a "surrounding belt of restriction" (Dworkin, 1977, p. 31). In discussing the doughnut ring, criminal justice scholar John Kleinig (1996, p. 3) explains that this model presents appropriate discretion as a relative phenomenon because "the standards relevant to judging exercises of discretion will . . . be relative to the norms that are implicit in that particular ring—the ring of norms governing legal, judicial, police, or other practice." To exacerbate matters, Kleinig continues, stating that discretion is not a "univocal concept," (1996, p. 3) meaning that not everyone speaks of discretion or conceptualizes it with the same words or in the same fashion.

Professor Kleinig is certainly correct that scholars of police discretion have yet to agree upon a universal definition of, or common philosophy about, the appropriate use of officer discretion. Normative viewpoints about the use of discretion abound, some agreeing and others conflicting. Thus, it is unlikely that any permanent consensus can be reached in this realm. Progress can be made in regard to understanding officer discretion by observing how it does operate rather than how it should operate.

Designing an empirical model of discretion requires that we revisit Dworkin's (1977) doughnut model. This model is useful because it demonstrates that discretion is bound by a ring of norms. However, this model is misleading in two key respects. First of all, with regard to any set of norms, discretion is bound by only one ring at a time in the doughnut model. This seems to suggest that any view of discretion must only consider one source of influence at a time. Secondly, assuming Dworkin's doughnuts are all the same size, the doughnut model suggests that each set of norms offers the exact same amount of space within the hole of discretion. That is, each set of norms provides the same boundary as the others.

Rather than looking at boundaries on discretion as an assortment of doughnuts, I suggest a single metaphor that will help capture the relative importance of each set of norms (boundaries) simultaneously. Here, rather than a doughnut, I suggest another visual image associated with police work: a target.

The target is a more useful metaphor for two reasons. First, the target's multiple rings allow us to represent multiple sets of norms or boundaries at once. Second, each ring's distance from the bull's-eye (discretion) allows us to represent the level of constraint each ring has upon officer discretion. Therefore, the outermost rings have the least ability to constrain discretion whereas the innermost rings have the most. It is important to note that though this model is useful, the distance of a given ring from the center of the target is not stagnant. For instance, an officer threatened with a lawsuit may begin to consider legal boundaries as more constraining than some other set of norms that once occupied a space close to the target's center.

This is also heartening for law enforcement managers because they may be able to help individual officers to rearrange rings (priorities) through training, emphasis, and other mechanisms. Thus, we can conceptualize a manager's struggle with the discretion used by officers as a struggle to impress his or her view of the discretion target upon the officers. The distance from the center that each manager attributes to a given set of norms tells a great deal about the level of importance the manager places upon each boundary.

Like most managers, local law enforcement managers must communicate their expectations of employee behavior via a written statement of their agency's standard operating procedures. However, the nature of the law enforcement profession makes it all but impossible to plan for every possible situation, thus making it necessary for officers to develop and use professional discretion on a daily basis (Goldstein, 1963; Lipsky, 1981). As a result, the use of discretion can sometimes undermine the written SOPs, the chain of command, and the ability of management to control frontline bureaucrats (Coe & Wiesel, 2001; Lipsky, 1981; Mastrofski, 2004; Maynard-Moody & Musheno, 2003).

This problem, according to Coe and Wiesel (2001, p. 726), reflects the idea that "police departments are a bit schizophrenic" because

> On the one hand, they are quasi-military organizations with a distinct chain of command and very detailed rules and regulations . . . [while] on the other hand, research has conclusively demonstrated the high degree of personal discretion exercised daily by police officers.

The root of this problem according to Davis (1996) surfaces when one considers the inescapable tradeoffs in managing members of every profession. Davis continues,

> A manager cannot have the advantages of someone's [professional] judgment and completely control what they decide. Insofar as someone must work to rule (that is, exercise only 'necessary discretion'), he cannot rule his work (have 'decisional autonomy'); insofar as he does rule his work, he cannot simply work to rule. If we agree that police officers know much that their superiors do not, and that we want that knowledge to enter appropriately into their decision making, we have already agreed that we do not want them to work to rule. If we want

their discretion . . . we must move away from the military style, command-and-control hierarchy of today's police organization. We must leave police room for (something like) professional judgment (Ibid., 1996, p. 29).

If we (scholars, practitioners, and the general population) agree that discretion is necessary, it makes sense that we want a deeper understanding of the ways in which discretionary decisions are made. Moreover, we may want to know whether rank influences these decision patterns. This book aims to help police managers, frontline officers, and scholars explore discretion by exposing readers to a detailed treatment of the components that make up discretionary choices, and how these components vary between frontline and command staff. In addition, this book is focused on real-world analysis and improvement of discretionary priorities for single and multiple agencies.

SUMMARY

As this chapter has illustrated, discretion is imperative in the realm of local law enforcement. Previous research on discretion revealed a host of variables which influence discretionary decision-making. More recent research has added to our awareness of other factors that affect discretion, such as race and gender, supervisorial influence, and voter demands (Briggs, 2013; Nowacki, 2011; Tasdoven & Kapucu, 2013; Regoeczi & Kent, 2014; Baldi & LaFrance, 2013). The Target Model presented herein is unique in that it allows the reader to assess the relative degree of influence each variable has on these choices. The next chapter will use in-depth interviews with police chiefs and sheriffs to argue that even in a command and control environment premised on standardization and uniformity, room for discretion is a necessity.

Chapter 2

Professional vs. Bureaucratic Accountability in Local Law Enforcement Management Decision-Making

Student Learning Outcomes	Practical Learning Outcomes
Students will be able to understand the use of discretion as an accountability tool.	Practitioners will be able to relate the use of discretion to managing expectations from a variety of sources.
Students will understand that accountability is nuanced and complex rather than dichotomous.	Practitioners will gain initial exposure to common sentiments about discretion from top managers in law enforcement agencies.
Students will begin to see how accountability research leads directly to the creation of the Target Model.	Practitioners will be able to relate their work to each category of the Target Model.
Students will deeply consider the relationship between rules and discretion.	Practitioners will appreciate the relationship between rules and discretion.
Students will begin to consider what their own discretionary decisions would look like.	Practitioners will be able to consider their own personal views of discretion.
Students will appreciate the pitfalls associated with being too rule-bound as well as those associated with having too much discretionary authority.	Practitioners will appreciate these same pitfalls.

An earlier version of this chapter appeared in *The Law Enforcement Executive Forum.* 10(1), 145-165.

Throughout their careers, public servants often find that their agencies' rules are not always compatible with the urges they feel as professionals seeking an optimal outcome with a given client (Maynard-Moody & Musheno, 2003). Expressed in terms of public administration scholars Barabra Romzek and Melvin Dubnick's (1987) accountability typology, this conflict occurs when professional accountability streams meet bureaucratic accountability streams in a worker's decision-making process. While common in many public agencies, this conflict has received notable attention in studies of law enforcement officers' decision-making behaviors (Lipsky, 1980; Mastrofski, 2004; Maynard-Moody & Musheno, 2003; Oberweis & Musheno, 1999).

Though the intersection of professional and bureaucratic accountabilities at the frontline of police operations has received much attention, examinations of this phenomenon at the apex of law enforcement organizations, especially county sheriffs' offices, are impressively scarce. This study, based on police chiefs and sheriffs' responses to a mock scenario that juxtaposes professional and bureaucratic accountabilities, is a preliminary attempt to explore this research void. The driving questions in this study are: When faced with the given scenario, to which form of accountability do law enforcement CEOs demonstrate allegiance? In making this choice, what differences in the responses of elected sheriffs and appointed police chiefs are attributable to the method of selection by which each manager obtained office and the antecedent variables that effect selection?

From the responses of police chiefs and county sheriffs, data from this exploratory study indicates a pervasive preference for bureaucratic accountability operationalized as an officer's adherence to the agency's SOP manual. Managers who chose this modal response cited three reasons for choosing adherence to the SOPs at the expense of professional discretion: (1) adherence to SOPs ensures agency coordination, (2) adherence to SOPs minimizes potential legal liability issues, and (3) adherence to SOPs is, in fact, an indication of a law enforcement agency's level of professionalism. The minority of respondents who chose to support an officer's professional discretion at the expense of adherence to SOPs cited two reasons for doing so: (1) the complexity of frontline law enforcement limits a written policy's specificity with regard to behavioral instructions in any given situation type, and (2) despite a common profession, each officer brings a unique personality and set of values to the workplace.

Before exploring this organizational malady, the reader must first understand arguments that support adherence to SOPs as well as arguments that champion the use of professional discretion. To this end, the reader may refer to the previous chapter.

EXPECTATIONS

I expect that law enforcement agencies proactively craft SOPs for two complementary reasons: (1) to articulate expectations in order to coordinate effort toward a common organizational end (positive reward perspective), and (2) to avoid legal sanctions (negative reward perspective) (Skinner, 1957).[1]

Whether a given policy is written out of a desire to earn a reward or to avoid punishment, it is impossible for even the most comprehensive policy to account for the unique nuances inherent in some of the situations a patrol officer or deputy sheriff might encounter. Police managers may keep this in mind and avoid placing too strong of an emphasis on SOPs in order to signal to their subordinates that individual choices are part and parcel of their job descriptions. Managers may also limit the degree to which they call attention to SOPs because doing so could leave subordinates feeling helpless or impotent in the absence of a clearly written directive. Finally, managers might seek to avoid creating an environment in which sociologist Robert Merton's (1940) notion of goal displacement flourishes.

Statements to this effect suggest that there is more to an officer's job than simply complying with an agency's policy manual; these statements highlight the need for some degree of professional autonomy, allowing the officer to make discretionary decisions based on the officer's particular expertise (Davis, 1996).

METHOD

As part of a larger project, the following study uses qualitative data obtained through in-depth interviews with twelve county sheriffs, four in Iowa, five in Illinois, three in Wisconsin, and sixteen municipal police chiefs in eight counties. This study explores the choice patterns of county sheriffs and municipal police chiefs elicited from their responses to a scenario that places professional autonomy at odds with bureaucratic accountability to the agencies' SOPs. Additionally, I will compare the justifications that sheriffs and chiefs use for making their choices. I will supplement these qualitative responses with nonparametric measures of association between several professionalism indicator variables (described below) and managers' responses.

---

1 A positive reward comes from the presentation of a desirable stimulus to encourage a behavior (agency cooperation), while a negative reward comes from the removal of an undesirable stimulus (lawsuits) to encourage a behavior (Skinner, 1957).

CASE SELECTION AND PROCESS

Cases were selected based on two criteria. First, in order to hold constant any regional effects on law enforcement decision-making, I used a purposive sampling method that targeted sheriffs and police chiefs in three Midwestern states. Second, in order to capture variation in decision-making based on agency size, I chose only counties with an urbanization index (*UI*) score of two or five.[2] (See Table 1).

I mailed cover letters, made phone calls, and sent emails to sixteen sheriffs and forty-three police chiefs. In the end, I successfully recruited twelve sheriffs (75% participation rate) and eighteen police chiefs (42% participation rate). Eight sheriffs came from UI-2 counties, and four sheriffs came from UI-5 counties. Fourteen police chiefs came from UI-2 counties, and four came from UI-5 counties. Once recruited, interviews were conducted in the managers' offices or via telephone.

Table 1: Urbanization Index Scores of Respondents[3]

County	Score
F	5
L	2
C	5
I	2
D	2
K	5
G	2
B	2
H	2
J	2
E	5
A	2

RESPONDENT CHARACTERISTICS AND VARIABLES OF INTEREST

Out of space considerations, the most pertinent data reflecting respondent characteristics appear in Table 2.[4] Most generally, all law

---

2 This indicator, according to Falcone & Wells (1995), is stacked in favor of chiefs because sheriffs are likely to have nonsworn personnel carrying out duties other than enforcement (e.g., detention, civil process, etc.).

3 2003 USDA Urban Influence Codes http://www.ers.usda.gov/Data/UrbanInfluenceCodes/2003/

4 Some smaller towns within UI-2 counties had as few as 10 employees. To account for these outliers, the medians are reported.

enforcement managers were males. All sheriffs were white, and only two chiefs were non-white (African-American). Of particular interest to this study are the professionalism indicator variables:

- the manager's education level
- the manager's professional training
- the manager's professional association memberships
- the ratio of sworn officers to total employees in the manager's agency
- the urban influence code of the manager's host county
- the accreditation of the agency

Table 2: Average Respondent Characteristics of Sheriffs and Chiefs

Demographics	Manager Type	
	Sheriff	**Police Chief**
Mean Age	**54** Range: 45-61	**51** Range: 38-64
Median County Residence (in years)	**46** Range: 24.5-61 years	**28** Range: 2 months-64 years
Median Years in Current Position	**7** Range: 1-16 years	**4** Range: 2 months-27 years
Median Years in Current Department	**26** Range: 1-40 years	**4** Range: 2 months-34 years
Median Total Years in LE	**31** Range: 20.5-40 years	**30** Range: 11-39 years
Median Total Employees	**183** Range: 46-558	**53** Range: 10-339
Median Sworn Officers	**58** Range: 17-449	**46** Range: 9-306
Level of Obtained Education	HS Diploma: 1 AA Degree: 2 BA Degree: 7 MA Degree: 2 PhD Degree: 0 JD Degree: 0	HS Diploma: 1 AA Degree: 1 BA Degree: 5 MA Degree: 6 PhD Degree: 1 JD Degree: 1

THE SCENARIO

Interviewees were asked to respond to the following scenario:

One of your investigators, Detective Marlowe, is known for the aggressive "old school" tactics that he employs during the course of his work on difficult cases. While he is one of your best officers, solving almost all of his assigned cases with a very laudable conviction ratio, some sergeants in your department disagree with his tactics because he often disregards standard operating procedures. Detective Marlowe does this, he claims, because "going by the book" hampers his ability to get his job done. He further argues the SOP fails to account for the specific demands and nuances of his investigative work. These sergeants are complaining that his behavior is unprofessional, citing the detective's lack of civility and the brash tone he takes with prisoners. These sergeants have asked for your advice. What would you say?

After listening to each manager's response, I followed up by explaining that the scenario was meant to juxtapose professional discretion against adherence to the agency's SOPs and then asked, "Which do you find more important?"

FINDINGS

Sheriffs' Responses

Ten of the twelve (83%) sheriffs expressed an overall preference for adhering to the SOPs at the cost of Detective Marlowe's professional discretion. The other two sheriffs expressed a preference for professional discretion, but only if the detective was acting legally (especially in terms of the constitutional rights of those with whom he deals) and ethically. Among those who gave the most common response, two suggested the SOPs include guidelines that deal with almost all possible variants of a given situation and could be amended to include unforeseen variants in the future. These same two sheriffs accorded the SOPs with the status of sacred organizational scripture. That is, to these two sheriffs, the SOPs are written orders directly from them. For instance, in his response to the scenario, one of these sheriffs said that he would bring Detective Marlowe in and say, "Why aren't you following *my* policies? These policies are written for a reason, and they're meant to be followed." (Note that the personal pronoun "my" shows the degree to which managers invest themselves, and their interests, in the policies.)

The other eight sheriffs expressed less ownership of the SOP manual and agreed that the manual could not be written in such a fashion as to cover every situation for a deputy. Six of these eight conceded that professional discretion has a very important role but only within the guidelines of the SOPs. In other words, many sheriffs felt that discretion is built into the SOPs, even if these policies are not situation specific.

When explaining his choice of bureaucratic accountability, another sheriff cited the need for teamwork and uniform responses to similar situations across all shifts saying, "It's very important that people aren't off doing their own thing because then you lose integrity in the department. You lose a sense of teamwork." This explanation most closely reflects Weber's perspective on the need for SOPs to maintain organizational order and progress toward shared goals. This sheriff went on to explain that, in addition to coordinating the entire agency, strict adherence to SOPs helps "curb rumors and prevent antagonism between officers on different shifts" and to "curb competition and animosity so that [the officers] can talk a lot about getting things done together and being part of a bigger picture." To reinforce this notion, the sheriff holds teambuilding retreats every six weeks with all forty-four members of his command staff so they can plan and communicate with one another.

Another two sheriffs explained that their preferences for adherence to the SOPs at the cost of professional discretion were based on maintaining a strong chain of command. These detectives were especially unnerved by Detective Marlowe because his supervisors complained about his defiant behaviors and apparent disregard for the chain of command.

Five of the twelve sheriffs cited the SOP manual's role in helping them to avoid legal sanctions. To them, the SOP manual is less focused on coordinating employees toward a common goal and more focused on avoiding legal liability. Yet another sheriff explained strict adherence to the SOPs as a political accountability mechanism saying, "We need to meet with [Det. Marlowe] to talk about why following policy is so important, particularly as it relates to oversight by the community . . . because that relates to their confidence in the sheriff's office." This sheriff went on to describe how bureaucratic accountability manifests itself as political accountability in his county stating:

> We reinforce our staff to follow policies and procedures because that's what we use to evaluate critiques from the community. . . One of the practices I put into place in 2007 when I took office was to place our policies, procedures, and regulations on our website.

This sheriff meets monthly with a community group, or township, in his county to talk about his agency's policies and procedures to ensure that they mesh well with "community expectations."

Two other sheriffs actually cited adherence to the SOP manual as more of a reflection of the agency's professionalism than the level of discretion used by an individual officer. One of these sheriffs, manager of an accredited agency, explained that his agency's SOPs are, in fact, professional standards of behavior. This response is thought provoking because it illuminates how a form of professional accountability, seeking and earning accreditation, requires an agency to create, implement, and uphold specific SOPs. In discussing the rigors imposed by the most common accreditation body, the Commission of Accreditation for Law Enforcement Agencies (CALEA), budgeting experts Charles Coe and Deborah Wiesel (2001, p. 726) assert that an agency has to "comply with over 400 standards."

Police Chiefs' Responses

The police chiefs' responses were slightly more variable than the sheriffs' responses; fourteen (78%) expressed a preference for adherence to SOPs while four (22%) expressed a preference for professional discretion. Of the fourteen who chose adherence to SOPs, many asserted that following agency policies is a manifestation of professionalism and cognizance of potential legal liability.

Citing legal liability as the driving force behind his preference for a strict enforcement of SOPs, one chief expressed disgust at the scenario, claiming that it is "out of television . . . not out of our experience." He further explained he felt this way because success could not come without following the SOPs, stating that, "Most of the policies and procedures help [an investigator] to stay within the boundaries that the court system has in place and help [the investigator] to make the best possible case." Similarly, another chief vehemently opposed the detective's behavior. The chief, relying on his deontological ethical view, identified results acquired through the detective's misbehavior as being "fruits of a poisonous tree." He went on to claim that,

> doing something that violates the constitutional rights of one of our clients or in such a way that you're bringing the department into disrepute, I don't really care about your results because they're poisonous. They aren't doing us any good. They may be causing us to have arrests, but they may be exposing us to other problems, far greater . . . If what he's doing is inappropriate, either legally or professionally, we're going to bring him into line and change his behavior.

Another chief intimated that he had been hired to command a department that did not have a standard operating procedure manual. This chief explained that he was the fourth police chief in this municipality since its initial creation in the 1800s, and the first chief to have been brought in from another city. Thus, he has helped the agency move its focus from non-codified institutional memory to formal written policies beginning with the most critical issues.

One chief, emphasizing the importance of adherence of to the SOPs, stated, "if [the detective is] violating the SOPs, then he's not being professional." Many others felt that sufficient discretion was written into the SOPs. One suggested that officers "can still have discretion without ignoring the SOPs . . . they can stay within those guidelines but achieve their goals with some of their discretion." According to another chief, this is not easily done:

> You'd like to think most SOPs have room for discretion . . . but when it's becoming obvious to other employees that that detective is going outside the SOPs, that's when it's time to look into it and take corrective action. That way, everybody's on the same page. That way, you don't have Detective Smith or Jones also going outside the SOPs and lose control [of your agency].

The following responses highlight the emphasis four chiefs placed upon the coordinating role of the SOPs and the need for enforcement of behavioral expectations. Here, one chief cited the importance of enforcing the agency's policies, saying

> If he is violating the SOPs, he needs to basically be drawn and quartered because once it comes to your attention that he is violating the SOP and you do nothing to him . . . that becomes the *new* SOP [emphasis added].

Another chief explained the need to look at practice versus policy, explaining:

> There's no sense in having an SOP if no one is going to follow it. If no one is following this SOP, but we're giving them so much discretion that is outside of it . . . we've got a bigger problem . . . How many other SOPs are people not following?

Two chiefs seemed personally offended by violations of departmental policy, demonstrating a great deal of ownership and reflecting the "sacred scripture" mentality mentioned in the case of the two sheriffs. One of these chiefs asserted, "The SOP [manual], as far as I'm concerned, is the standard by which I direct my people in written form." Another expressed a desire to "make it clear [to Detective Marlowe]" that the SOPs reflect the "expectations of the department and myself [sic]."

As was the case for sheriffs who chose professional discretion, police chiefs who made the same choice were quick to point out that they would only support discretion if it met legal and ethical standards (though not necessarily policy standards). The main themes that surfaced when these chiefs explained their collective preference for professional discretion over strict adherence to the SOPs were the complexity of the law enforcement landscape and the vast amount of personality differences among their officers. Exemplifying the former theme, one chief asserted:

> You might have a policy and procedure that says to do this, this, and this . . . but in real life situations, when it's a chaotic mix of personalities and different things occurring in that investigation, sometimes you can't just take it from top down and go one, two, three, four.

Demonstrating the latter theme, another chief claimed:

> [While] there are some hard and fast rules that can't be deviated from . . . in the scenario you mentioned, I think discretion is in order. Each investigator is different in their approach to how they do the job. As long as the behavior is ethical and not violating the law, and [the officer is] successful in getting [his] job done, I would allow for that discretion and let him deviate from the SOP.

Sheriffs versus Chiefs

Initial results from this exploratory study indicate that sheriffs and police chiefs overwhelmingly enforce adherence to their agencies' written policies at the expense of professional discretion. Justifications for these preferences are very similar for each type of manager (see Table 4). As expected, SOPs are considered important components of organizational coordination and teamwork. Also as expected, SOPs are often considered safeguards in terms of legal liability. Quite unexpectedly, however, adherence to the SOPs is considered by most managers in this study to be a greater indication of professionalism than the use of professional discretion. It is also important to note that a great many issues were inferred from a very simple scenario. There was no mention in the scenario of Detective Marlowe violating any law, much less the constitutional rights of those with whom he interacts. Still, many managers inferred that this was a possibility, whether as a reason for or a result of his violation of the SOPs. This shows that local law enforcement managers are so keenly aware of legal liability issues that even the faintest hint of liability is unacceptable. Indeed, sheriffs and police chiefs commonly mentioned how litigious Americans have become in their responses. Sheriffs seemed even more emphatic about avoiding legal liability perhaps because of the enhanced functional scope of most sheriffs' offices (i.e., rather than simply doing patrol and enforcement, most sheriffs also serve civil papers, provide court security, and most importantly, supervise incarcerated inmates in the county jail). This broad scope manifests liability on multiple fronts at any given moment.

While only a handful of agencies in the study were accredited, it is interesting to note that most managers of unaccredited agencies did not express a pessimistic view of accreditation. Much to the contrary, most managers lamented that they did not have adequate resources (human or financial) or facilities to obtain accreditation. In fact, many managers explained that they reaped the benefits of accreditation by "borrowing" from the policy manual of nearby accredited agencies. Others chose less expensive and less demanding methods of revising SOPs such as contracting with risk management companies or hiring law firms to review their policies.

Despite the majority of managers who supported accreditation, there were a few who resented it. Some were resentful of the many law enforcement managers who develop relationships with an accreditation body and upon retirement actually work for that body. Others complained that accreditation standards are too constraining; one manager cited the control accreditation placed over even the type of undershirt officers may wear beneath their uniform. Others also complained that the resources needed for accreditation could be used in more meaningful ways in specific jurisdictions. Ultimately, some felt that accreditation is unnecessary if a manager develops a policy manual and maintains a vigilant watch over it.

Of the four chiefs managing accredited agencies, three indicated a preference for bureaucratic accountability. At first this presents an interesting intellectual challenge because accreditation seems to be a mechanism by which an agency shows accountability to the profession rather than to the hierarchy and rules of the agency; however, a cursory view of accreditation standards shows that an accreditation body (the most frequently mentioned was CALEA) dictates the exact wording of an agency's SOPs in order to ensure uniformity (See Appendix A). Thus, one could argue that this is an instance in which bureaucratic accountability is a means by which an agency demonstrates its professional accountability to the accreditation body. If this is the case, a traditional notion of professional accountability as deference to expertise seems to conflict with this neo-professional accountability to bureaucratized accreditation bodies. This apparent conflict, while beyond the scope of the present book, needs to be studied. Then again, of the twelve non-accredited agencies, nine expressed this same preference for bureaucratic accountability.

Table 3: Sheriffs' & Police Chiefs' Responses to the Scenario

Response	County Sheriff Code	City Police Chief Code
Bureaucratic Accountability (Adherence to SOPs)	A, B, C, D, G, H, I, J, K, L	A1, A2, B1, B2, D2, F1, F2, G1, G2, I1 JI, L1, L3, L4
Professional Accountability (Deference to Professional Discretion)	E, F	D1, E1, E2, L2

Table 4: Role of SOPs

	Sheriffs	Police Chiefs
Protection from Legal Liability	5	2
Agency Coordination	1	4
Ensure Political Accountability	1	0
Control from Command Staff	2	3
SOPs ensure Professionalism	2	1
Discretion built into SOPs	2	3

*Some managers cited more than one role for SOPs, while some cited none.

Correlates of Managers' Choices

I evaluated measures of association between the professional indicator variables and the managers' responses (see Table 5). For dichotomous by dichotomous measures, I will report Pearson's *phi*. For dichotomous by ordinal measures, I will report Spearman's *rho*. For dichotomous by interval or ratio measures, I will report Pearson's *R*. Each of these are statistical tests used to determine the strength of the relationship between two variables. (You may find it useful to refer to an introductory statistics textbook if unfamiliar with these measures of association.) In the section that follows, I will evaluate each proposition in turn.

Table 5: Correlates of Choice: Professional Autonomy vs Adherence to SOPs†

Professionalism Indicator Variables	Preference for Professional Autonomy (1, 0)
Education	NS
Total Training	NS
Local Academy Training (1,0)	.734***
State Academy Training (1,0)	-.553**
National Academy Training (1,0)	-.310 (p<.10, >.05)
National Workshops (1,0)	NS
Total Professional Association Memberships	NS
Local Association Membership (1,0)	NS
State Sheriff's Association Membership (1,0)	NS
State Police Association Membership (1,0)	NS
National Association Membership (1,0)	-.373*
IACP Membership (1,0)	NS
NSA Membership (1,0)	NS
NACOP Membership (1,0)	NS
Sworn Employees/Total Employees	NS
Accreditation (1,0)	NS
Urbanization Index	.526**
Sheriff or Chief (1,0)	NS

Phi (dichotomous), Spearman's Rho (Ordinal), and Pearson's R (Interval/Ratio) Correlations

†Adherence to SOPs is coded to be the exact opposite of Deference to Professional Autonomy, thus a negative (-) correlation suggests that the independent variable is associated with adherence to SOPs.

* = p<.05; **=p<.01; ***=p<.001

Proposition 1: Managers with higher education levels and more professional training are expected to favor their officers' use of professional discretion over adherence to SOPs.

No significant relationship exists between education level and a manager's choice of professional or bureaucratic accountability among managers in this sample. Similarly, total training (the sum of local academy, state academy, national academy, national workshops, and other training) does not seem to co-vary with a manager's preference. Some individual types of training, however, do share a relationship with managers' choices. A manager who has attended a local academy may be more inclined to prefer professional discretion at the expense of adherence to SOPs (phi = .734, significant at the .001 p-level). However, a manager who has attended a state academy is more likely to prefer adherence to SOPs (phi = -.553, significant at the .01 p-level). For those managers who attended a national academy, the relationship between training and a preference for professional discretion is in the unexpected (negative) direction, though the relationship is insignificant (p<.10, but >.05).

Proposition 2: The total number of state, local, and national professional associations to which a manager belongs will co-vary with the manager's willingness to choose professional discretion over adherence to SOPs.

No significant relationship exists between the total number of professional associations (local, state, or national associations) to which a manager belongs and his preference of bureaucratic or professional accountability. When looking at each type of professional association, the only significant correlate of a manager's preference of professional accountability was membership in a national association, and this relationship was in the opposite direction than proposed (phi= -.373, significant at the .05 p-level).

Proposition 3: Managers who prize professional accountability are expected to be more easily found in agencies with a higher ratio of sworn officers.

Contrary to my expectation, no significant relationship exists between the ratio of sworn officers in a manager's agency and his or her preference for professional accountability.

Proposition 4: Managers in larger counties (with an urban influence code of two) will give more deference to professional discretion than managers in smaller counties (with an urban influence code of five).

There is a significant relationship between a manager's preference of professional autonomy and the urban influence code of the manager's host county; however, this relationship is significant in the opposite direction than proposed. Smaller county size (higher urban influence code) rather than larger county size (smaller urban influence code) is positively associated with a manager's preference for professional accountability (phi = .526, significant at the .01 p-level). My speculation is that more rural counties with higher UI codes are more remote, making it more difficult for supervisors to respond on scene than might be the case in geographically dense urban areas.

Proposition 5: Managers of accredited agencies will be more likely to choose professional discretion than adherence to SOPs.

No significant relationship exists between accreditation and a manager's preference for adherence to SOPs or allowing for officer discretion.

Discussion and Reconsideration of Propositions

The preliminary data collected for this study does not support any of the five propositions made. In fact, some measures of association reach statistical significance in the opposite direction than expected.

A manager's education level shows no association with his choice of bureaucratic or professional accountability. Similarly, a manager's total training does not seem to be associated with his scenario response, national academy training, or participation in national workshops. Perhaps a larger, random sample of sheriffs and police chiefs may show relationships, but no conclusions can be drawn from the present data.

Some types of training, however, do seem to influence a manager's preference for adhering to SOPs or allowing officer discretion. Training at a local academy is significantly associated with a preference for professional discretion, but training at a state academy is significantly associated with a preference for adherence to SOPs. These conclusions lead me to ask: What differences in local and state academy training might influence differences in managers' preferences? There is no known study of curricular differences between each type of academy, but the data show that curricular differences might not be the intervening variable of interest. Instead, a county's urban influence code seems to be the intervening variable.

Managers in counties with a larger urban influence code (smaller counties) are significantly more likely to attend a local academy. These managers are also significantly more likely to prefer an officer's use of discretion over adherence to SOPs. Conversely, managers in UI-2 (smaller urban influence code) counties seem to prefer adherence to SOPs, and these same managers are more likely to have attended a state academy. While I find it difficult to explain why managers in smaller counties are more likely to attend local academies, I can theorize about the relationship between county size and a manager's preference for professional discretion.

On average, managers in UI-2 counties have a median of 133 employees, sixty-seven of whom are sworn officers. The median number of employees for a UI-5 manager in the sample is fifty-five, thirty-two of whom are sworn officers. Thus, sheriffs and chiefs in smaller counties generally manage fewer employees (though there are some exceptions; see note 3), so they and others in their command staff may be better able to oversee their officers' use of discretion more easily. This happens, according to criminal justice expert Victor Sims (1988), because supervisors in smaller law enforcement agencies work within a more realistic span of control than supervisors in larger agencies. In his study of small town and rural police, Sims argues that smaller departments are less likely to be organized as impersonal bureaucracies and are more likely to foster collegiality between supervisors and subordinates. Furthermore, Sims (1988, p. 131) argues, discretion is fundamentally different in small and large agencies.

> [In large agencies,] Bureaucracies establish and enforce detailed guidelines. If an officer encounters certain checklist items, policy dictates that the officer must respond with a certain disposition. The bureaucracy polices by controlling the actions and reactions of the individual officer in the field. The bureaucracy cannot give the officer discretionary power because to do so would mean the bureaucracy relinquishes policing power to the individual. The patrol officer on the large police department acts not so much as a bureaucrat but as a mechanic for the bureaucracy.

In comparison, Sims (1988, p. 131) argues,

> [T]he small town philosophy relies on the individual officer to provide the full range of police services. Small towners and ruralites expect the officer to use and display discretion, make judgment calls, and police. They expect personal, individualized, custom-designed policing. Small town philosophy mandates that all community members share in the responsibility for policing, but community members delegate the authority of police discretion to the police. The small town or rural community trusts the individual officer enough to expect him to use discretion. The patrol officer on the small town or rural police department acts not so much as a social mechanic but as a public servant.

Simply stated, this view of officer discretion holds that an agency's reliance on SOPs at the expense of discretion increases with the agency's size. This leads me to believe that the fundamental flaw in my propositions is based on the two different definitions of professionalism in the scholarly community: the Criminal Justice field perspective that professionalism is having SOPs versus the perspective of Public Administration scholars that professionalism pertains to being an expert and, thus, not only able but expected to use discretion; these perspectives can cause misunderstandings between scholars in each field. To Romzek and Dubnick (1987), professionalism is marked by expertise, and professional accountability is expressed by deferring to the expertise and discretion of the individual officer.

To many managers in my study, this was almost antithetical to their definition of professionalism, which incorporates standardization of behavior to allow for coordination of the agency and to minimize legal liability. This may explain why many managers feel that the pinnacle of law enforcement professionalism is reached through accreditation. A cursory visit to the website of the CALEA seems to echo this view of professionalism. Here, CALEA extols the virtues of gaining accreditation, citing the requirement that "an agency . . . develop a comprehensive, well thought out, uniform set of written directives," (SOPs) which, in turn, will "facilitate an agency's pursuit of *professional excellence*" (CALEA, 2008; See Appendix A for a list of these written directives from the CALEA website).

Such statements hint that law enforcement professionalization as defined by the profession is really about standardization and bureaucratization. If this is the case, one may reconsider Romzek and Dubnick's view of professional accountability or at least try to find some means by which to reconcile these disparate views of professionalism.

Unresolved Questions and Future Research

While this study demonstrates that SOPs serve the purposes of coordinating an organization's employees and limiting legal liability, these findings are old news. A more recent finding rests in the notion of adherence to organizational policies as a mechanism of professional accountability. That is, the distinction between these two accountability streams seems to blur in the responses of many managers and agency protocols and essentially become professional standards. This raises the question of whether professional standards and the bodies that create them have become so bureaucratized that managers perceive them to be forms of super-bureaucratic accountability from an external source of control. Or, perhaps, compliance with SOPs becomes a manifestation of political accountability (in the broadest conception thereof) to one's professional peers and oversight bodies. These considerations merit future research and show that the phenomenon of public sector accountability may be more complex at the county and municipal levels than at the federal level.

BACK TO THE TARGET RANGE

The first steps in the necessary future research, mentioned above, may come from the use of the Target Model of Discretion, presented earlier. The immediate question with regard to the Target Model, centers on the idea that frontline law enforcement officers may place greater emphasis on some rings while law enforcement CEOs place greater emphasis on others. If this is the case, defining appropriate boundaries of discretion may be facilitated by managers' attempts to change the rings on the officers' target so that the targets overlap and boundary priorities are given equal consideration.

SO WHAT?

This model may also help answer the "So what?" question in that it can be easily understood and applied by law enforcement practitioners. The target metaphor may also be a helpful icebreaker in teambuilding meetings and training sessions bent on sharing managers' views about discretion. For instance, a chief or sheriff can pass out blank targets and have officers fill them in by allocating ring values to different sets of norms or boundaries (e.g., legal liability, personal values, etc.). The manager can then present his or her own target, creating an atmosphere conducive to discussing different boundary sets and their relative weights. This is the logic underlying the following chapters in which the Target Model is presented as a diagnostic tool and later used as the basis of three case studies.

OPPORTUNITY FOR REFLECTION

For the following scenarios and questions, you may also use a Think, Pair, Square, Share approach to further discussion:

- Think individually about your answers
- Pair with a partner and exchange your responses
- Square combining two of these pair for further discussion
- Share the key points from your group's discussion to the whole class or squad room

What is the relationship between rules and discretion like in your agency or classroom?

Think of a situation where a superior (commanding officer, professor, or teacher) has given very specific rules for an assignment (e.g., a very detailed rubric, template, etc.), and compare that to a situation where the given instructions seemed to be too vague. With which assignment were you more comfortable? If you were frustrated in either case, did you communicate your frustration? How? What would it take to make you feel more at ease in discussing your reaction with your peers or superior/instructor?

What are some consequences of officers or students becoming too focused on following rules? What are the consequences of officers or students making autonomous discretionary decisions too often?

What would a personalized version of the Target Model look like for a recent decision you made in your career, studies, or personal life?

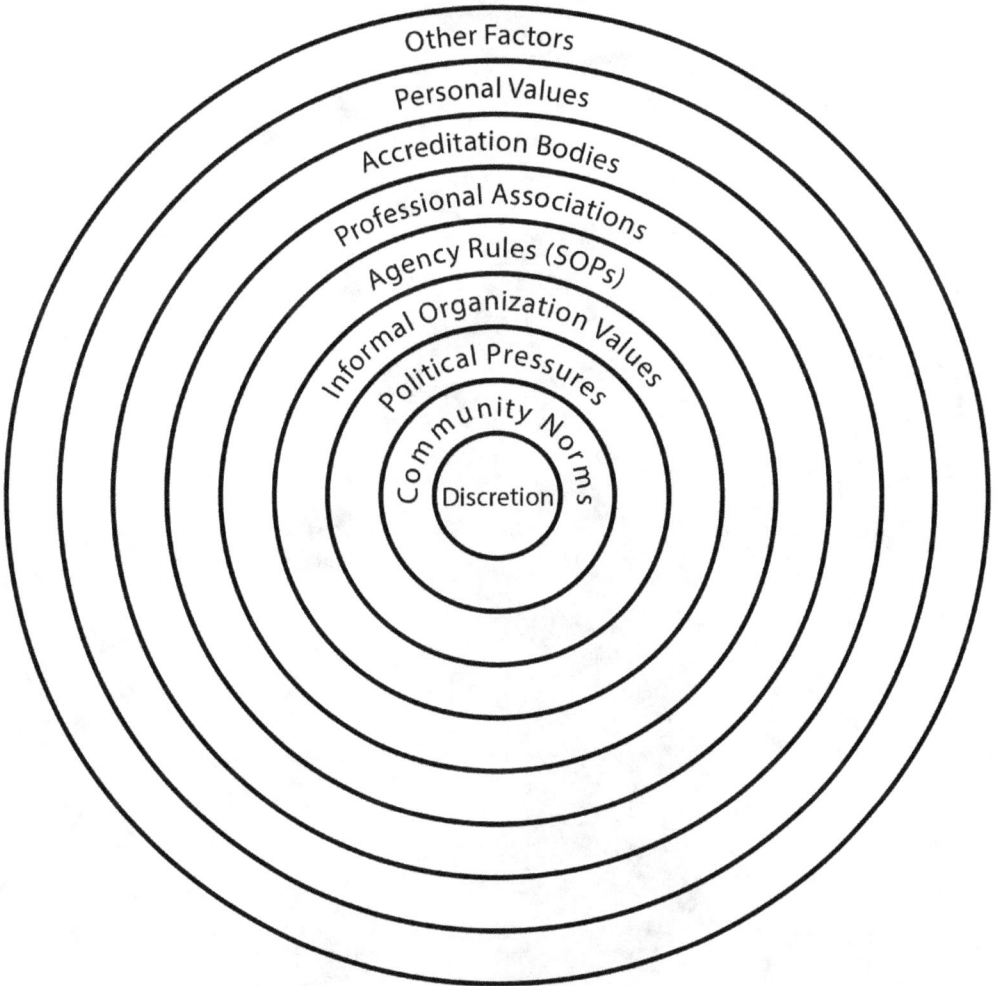

Figure 1: The Target Model of Discretion[1]

---

1 This image visually represents the Target Model of Discretion. The bull's-eye symbolizes discretion. Each influence on discretion is represented as a ring around the bull's-eye. The relative distance of a ring highlights the priority a respondent ascribes to one of nine potential factors known to guide the use of discretion. This is one possible way the factors could be arranged, but responses will vary depending on respondent's placement of priorities on a blank target.

Part II

Chapter 3

Visiting the Firing Range: Case Studies Using the Target Model of Discretion

Student Learning Outcomes	Practical Learning Outcomes
Students will gain appreciation of real world applicability of the Target Model in multiple settings.	Practitioners will be able to discuss findings from other agencies and compare those to what they would expect in their own respective agencies.
Students and Practitioners will engage in role-play activities as organization development consultants.	
Students and Practitioners will be able to consider the findings of these interventions and discuss how differences between rank levels may have emerged and may be solved.	

Earlier versions of each of these case studies appeared in the following volumes:

Case 1:
LaFrance, Casey (2010). Back to the Firing Range: An Exploratory Test of the Target Model of Discretion. Law Enforcement Executive Forum, 10(4), pp. 167-174.

Case 2:
LaFrance, Casey (2011). Targeting Discretion: An Exploration of Organizational Communication Between Rank Levels In A Medium Sized Southern U.S. Police Department. International Journal of Police Science and Management, 13(2), pp. 158-172.

Case 3:
LaFrance, Casey (2011). Rank and Discretionary Priorities in Forgottonia: Targeting Discretion in the Western Illinois/Eastern Iowa Region. Law Enforcement Executive Forum, 11(2), pp.79-85.

INTRODUCTION

In this chapter, the reader will see three concrete applications of the Target Model. The first two cases highlight the model's use as a diagnostic tool for individual agencies. The third case demonstrates the model's utility in multi-agency research and training settings. After presenting the results from each case and discussing the planned intervention techniques for the case, the reader will be given a series of questions to consider. The data collection process (survey distribution to both frontline officers and command staff members) is identical for each case. Simply, command staff members and frontline officers were provided with a blank, multi-ringed target and asked to rank the priority they give to each of nine variables (Community Norms, Personal Values, Informal Organization Norms, Other Managers, SOPs, Legal Liability, Professional Associations, Accreditation Bodies, and Political Pressures) when making discretionary choices. The mean responses of each group were then compared. Please see Chapter 5 for a more thorough discussion of the methodology employed. Specific details regarding participant numbers and the ratio of frontline officers to command staff members in each case will be provided as each case is presented.

CASE ONE: SINGLE MIDWESTERN AGENCY

This case involves a municipal police agency in a small Midwest-ern city with a population of around 20,000. This department has seven command staff members (ranging from the rank of sergeant to the rank of chief). All command staff members agreed to participate, yielding a 100% participation rate among top managers. Of the 21 frontline officers, 15 agreed to participate (71% of frontline officers).

Results: Case One

Analysis of responses from command staff members and frontline officers revealed a remarkable amount of similarity in the order that each group ranked the potential sources of influence (See Tables 6 and 7). Both groups rated agency rules and standard operating procedures as the most important determinants of discretionary behavior. Both groups also agreed that personal values (individual morality) serve as the second most important source of discretionary behavior, though command staffers ranked legal liability concerns equally with personal values and frontline officers ranked legal liability fourth overall. Most impressively, there was only one category that yielded a significant mean difference between frontline officers and command staff members. Top managers and patrol officers collectively agreed that informal organization values and peer group norms made up the fifth most important category. Individual rankings led to a significant mean difference (4.2 for frontline officers vs. 6 for command staffers; t=2.13, p=.052) between these two groups. Thus, frontline officers in this agency are apt to consider informal organizational values to be 4.2 rings away from the bull's-eye of a discretion target, while top managers on average rate the importance of this source of influence to be 6 rings away from the bull's-eye.

Table 6: Frontline Officers' Response Ranks

Measure	Mean Distance from Bull's-eye	Median Distance from Bull's-eye
Agency Rules	2.13 (#1)	2.00
Personal Values	2.66 (#2)	2.00
Community Norms	3.46 (#3)	3.00
Legal Liability	3.66 (#4)	3.00
Informal Organization Values	4.2 (#5)	4.00
Other Managers	4.66 (#6)	4.00
Professional Assoc.	5.93 (#7)	7.00
Political Pressure	6.33 (#8)	7.00
Accreditation	6.6 (#9)	8.00

Table 7: Command Staff Members' Response Ranks

Measure	Mean Distance from Bull's-eye	Median Distance from Bull's-eye
Agency Rules	2.00 (#1)	2.00
Personal Values	2.43 (#2 tie)	2.00
Community Norms	3.14 (#3)	3.00
Legal Liability	2.43 (#2 tie)	1.00
Informal Organization Values	6.00 (#5)	5.00
Other Managers	5.00 (#4)	5.00
Professional Assoc.	7.14 (#8)	8.00
Political Pressure	6.57 (#6)	6.00
Accreditation	7 (#7)	8.00

Discussion

With the exception of one determinant of discretion, there were no statistically significant differences between the discretionary priorities of command staff members and frontline officers. In simpler terms, this indicates that the command staff members of the department are effective in communicating discretionary priorities and ingraining these priorities into the daily lives of their subordinate officers. It is possible this behavior is modeled or is part of the department's training curriculum; however, frontline officers and command staff members in this agency do not agree on the importance of the agency's informal organizational culture in shaping discretionary decisions. Frontline officers are significantly more likely than their supervisors to cite the importance of informal organizational mechanisms that factor into their decisions regarding the appropriate use of discretion. It is important to address this issue, as the informal organization can often be as important to the health of an agency as the formal organization (Mayo, 1933; 1949; Barnard, 1938; Simon, 1947; Likert, 1961; 1967).

BE THE CONSULTANT

Before reading the analysis section for this case study, put yourself in the shoes of the consultant/researcher. Given the two tables above, how would you:

1. Explain why there might be differences between rank levels?
2. Address the underlying cause(s) of these differences?
3. Offer an action plan for the managers and subordinates?

Find a partner and compare your strategies.

What is the Informal Organization?

Scholars and organization development specialists use the term "informal organization" to encapsulate norms, values, language, and reward or punishment structures that are not formally articulated by management or incorporated in agency policy manuals (Barnard, 1938). Essentially, the informal organization develops as a result of employing human beings rather than automatons to perform public services (Maslow, 1947; McGregor, 1960). The existence of an informal organization is essential to the health of any agency, as it is impossible to codify every aspect of operations (Lipsky, 1980). For each individual in the agency, the informal organization helps to satisfy belongingness needs, giving each team member a sense of fitting in (Maslow, 1947). Additionally, the informal organization facilitates crucial components necessary in teamwork: trust, a spirit of common mission, and an awareness of how "we do things around here" (Golembiewski, 1972). The informal organization also helps employees receive immediate signals regarding appropriate or inappropriate behavior (Roethlisberger & Dickson, 1939). These signals come in the form of peer group sanctions, rewards, and punishments (mockery, ostracism, etc.) that are unaccounted for in the typical incentive or sanctions schedule formally articulated in the agency's policy manual (Mayo, 1933; 1949).

The Effects of Peer Group Bonding: Communication

Peer group bonding is an important source of support in the stressful environment of law enforcement. Beyond enhancing a sense of safety and belonging, peer bonds serve the overlooked role of making work more enjoyable. Because of the informal organization's important role in guiding peers toward common goals, no reasonable person would advocate for its abolition. Any attempt to eradicate the informal organization would likely lead to an even greater amount of peer group bonding (Hirschman, 1970). Managers, then, must respect the informal organization while focusing on curbing some of its less desirable effects, such as miscommunication, hyperbole, and sensationalism. These negative consequences are especially apparent when one considers that the average patrol officer spends a great deal more time interacting with peers than time spent with supervisors, especially managers at the apex of the organization.

Addressing Communication

When officers on the street are not perfectly informed of their commanders' intentions, these officers are more apt to try to guess them. Therefore, the first step in minimizing any negative effects of the informal organization is to ensure that as much information as possible is honestly and clearly presented to each member of the agency. While a manager may not always be capable of preventing incorrect information from spreading throughout the agency, the manager should make every effort to address false rumors (Houmanfar & Johnson, 2004). This is especially pertinent during periods of organizational change, such as the alteration of department policy (Bordia, et. al., 2006; DiFonzo & Bordia, 1998). The manager will be in a better position to react quickly to false information if the manager makes himself available for questions and comments from subordinates, or by having an "open door policy" (Blackburn & Rosen,

1993). Another proactive method to minimize misinformation in the informal organization is to spend time outside of one's office in the patrol car and in the office with subordinates or with "management by walking around" (Peters & Waterman, 2004; Serrat, 2009; Brandt, 1992; Blackburn & Rosen, 1993). Both of these mechanisms are designed to enhance trust between levels of the agency so that management and line workers are able to have open, honest discussions with one another regarding the work that is done by the agency.

Incorporating Informal Organizational Components into Department-Wide Communication

Perhaps evident to the reader, practicing management by walking around (MBWA) and having an open door policy are really recommendations for members of the agency's command staff to plug into the informal organization. Additional measures for achieving this goal can be found in the management literature. Based on scholarship on informal organizations (Barnard, 1938) and organization development (Schein, 1969) and my own research and experience, the following suggestions might be most appropriate:

1. Managers may consider the use of a liaison system in which frontline officers elect a peer to share information, concerns, and questions with command staff members.
2. Additionally, managers may consider an anonymous suggestion box, or its electronic equivalent (discussion board, etc.), as a way to elicit sentiments from subordinate officers.
3. Managers may attempt various team-building exercises with the assistance of an experienced organization development interventionist.
4. Managers may consider ride-alongs, one-on-one and small group meals, and other experiences aimed at getting to know each frontline officer and addressing each officer's questions and concerns.
5. In order to "humanize" command staff members, managers may try family outings, picnics, and other activities that allow the human side of the manager and the frontline employees to show through.
6. More formally, managers may invest in a superior-subordinate mentorship program through which a command staff member serves as a mentor for a handful of frontline officers. This is an appropriate continuation of department-sponsored mentorship

that too often ends abruptly after the FTO (field training officer) experience. These mentor-mentee groups also make for ideally sized training groups, provided each command staffer is willing to add training to his or her responsibilities.

7. While proactive intervention is essential to a healthy agency, reflection on management's and subordinate's behavior and decisions is also important. These are necessary after a particularly good or bad decision has been made by a member of the agency. Here, the mentorship described above may become an integral part of honest, open reflection. Questions to be used in these sessions may include: How did we handle this situation? Was there a conflicting message between command staffers and officers? What do we like/dislike about the decision(s) that we made? Would we act the same way in the future? Why or why not?

8. Another possible route to instilling trust and communication into the agency may be through the use of scenario-based training. Here, managers and subordinates may read, view, or experience a scenario and then describe, or demonstrate their individual reactions to each scenario. Then, managers and subordinates can see if their reactions match or if there is a disparity in these reactions. If the latter is true, managers and subordinates can then discuss the root(s) of these differences in reaction and come to a consensus regarding the appropriate reaction.

9. Human nature is such that officers may derive comfort from knowing that a resource is available to them regardless of whether or not they use it. With this in mind, it may be beneficial to the agency if command staffers take turns being "on call" for emergency and non-emergency questions from subordinates that cannot be answered by their immediate supervisors.

Finally, it is appropriate for the agency to take some time every so often to re-evaluate operations. Such opportunities present themselves in yearly milestones (budget planning, strategic planning sessions, evaluation of employee and group performance, etc.) and will help to address agency norms and customs, especially those that are undesirable. Here, managers and frontline officers need to remember that just because a behavior, or pattern of behavior, has become "normal," it is not always the most appropriate (some norms are not helpful to the organization) and to remember to avoid "goal displacement," a phenomenon where the agency's mission and attendant goals are lost in pursuit of following agency rules (Merton, 1940).

Management Reactions to These Suggestions

When presented with these suggestions, the chief in this case study tended to agree with them. In fact, his succinct reply reads in full:

> I have noticed some of the things you have pointed out and actually have been doing more MBWA. We also have a department picnic scheduled for next month and a policemen's ball in November. Your summary supports what I have been relaying to my staff.

The police department in this study appears to have taken pains to ensure that management priorities are communicated effectively with frontline officers. Frontline officers and command staff tend to agree when considering appropriate priorities in regards to the use of discretion. However, evidence suggests that command staffers can do more to consider and address the informal organization (peer group bonds, peer incentives, unspoken/unwritten rules of conduct) within which they operate. The case study presented above offers some specific suggestions that may enable command staff members to cultivate an awareness of the informal organization and respond appropriately to its demands.

CASE TWO: SOUTHERN POLICE DEPARTMENT

This case centers on a medium-sized local police department in a Georgia town with approximately 20,000 residents. The assistant chief of police agreed to ask his officers to participate in the project. In total, 20 employees participated in the survey: 12 were frontline officers, and 8 were members of the agency's command staff. Once data was collected, I conducted two-tailed, independent sample t-tests in order to ascertain the statistically significant differences in discretionary priorities between the two groups.

Results: Case Two

The study's findings are grouped in two separate sections. First, I will present specific findings and organization development ideas for the department that serves as the example case. Second, I will present general findings regarding the efficacy of the Target Model of Discretion as a theoretical device and an organization development tool.

Table 8: Frontline Officers' Response Ranks

Measure	Mean	Median
Agency Rules	1.5 (#1)	1.5
Legal Liability	3.0 (#4)	2.5
Personal Values	1.86** (#2)	2.0
Community Norms	4.17** (#5)	4.0
Informational Organizational Values	5.0 (#6)	5.0
Other Managers	2.91 (#3)	3.0
Professional Associations	5.67 (#7)	6.0
Political Pressures	6.92* (#9)	7.0
Accreditation Bodies	5.9 (#8)	5.0
Other	-	-

*p<0.10, **p<0.05

Table 9: Command Staff Members' Response Ranks

Measure	Mean	Median
Agency Rules	1.2 (#1)	1.0
Legal Liability	1.8 (#2)	2.0
Personal Values	4.20** (#4)	3.0
Community Norms	5.5** (#6)	5.0
Informational Organizational Values	6.67 (#9)	6.0
Other Managers	4.0 (#3)	4.0
Professional Associations	6.5 (#8)	6.5
Political Pressures	5.75* (#7)	5.0
Accreditation Bodies	5.0 (#5)	6.0
Other	-	-

*p<0.10, **p<0.05

Department-Specific Findings

This department exhibits well-developed communication patterns regarding the appropriate use of officer discretion. Command staff members and frontline officers agreed on the priority level of most of the variables offered as potential sources of constraint on officer discretion. However, the study uncovered significant differences in the priority level of three possible constraints on discretion: political pressures, community norms, and personal values. I will discuss the potential implications of these differences as well as their origins. For each issue, I will offer suggestions to remedy the disparity in perceived importance between levels of management. Prior to doing so, consider the following activity and questions in "Be the Consultant:"

BE THE CONSULTANT

Before reading the findings for this case study, put yourself in the shoes of the consultant/researcher. Given the two tables above, how would you:

1. Explain why there might be differences between rank levels?
2. Address the underlying causes of these differences?
3. Offer an action plan for managers and subordinates?

Find a partner and compare your strategies.

Political Pressures

Aggregate department responses reveal a minor though statistically significant ($t = -1.8$; $p = 0.094$, two-tailed test) inconsistency in the perceived importance of political pressures between managers and line workers. Managers placed political pressures almost two rings closer to the metaphorical discretionary bull's-eye than their subordinate officers (See Tables 8 and 9). The reader may soundly argue that such a difference is to be expected given that one crucial component of local government management is dealing with political pressures and, perhaps more importantly, insulating frontline workers as much as possible from local politics. However, managers may gain more respect and admiration from their subordinates by candidly commenting on affairs in the political realm of their municipality (Trautman, 2003). This course of action is especially encouraged if political pressures have a demonstrable effect on department policies, resource allocation, or decision processes. Such transparent communication may serve to reveal the origins of and rationale behind organizational changes to frontline officers. This, in turn, can enhance buy-in among frontline officers, facilitating smoother transitional periods. Another positive effect of communicating political pressures down the hierarchy of the agency is that doing so may serve to reinforce the often underappreciated roles that one's agency plays in each stage of the policy process.

<u>Specific Organization Development Exercises</u>

In order to reconcile the discrepancy regarding political pressures, command staff members may consider encouraging frontline officers to develop a greater understanding of how their municipality's government is structured and how elected officials and the city manager communicate their wishes to agency heads. To this end, the department may consider offering training sessions on these topics as well as suggesting that officers attend city government meetings on a regular basis. The latter activity may help officers identify and understand the perspectives of key constituencies and groups in the city, and help them keep pace with the ever-changing policy landscape in their city.

<u>Overall Priority Level: Low</u>

As managers and frontline officers agreed, political pressures are far removed from immediate influence on the use of discretion. This dimension of discretionary choice merits only a slight degree of concern for command staff.

Community Norms

Aggregate department responses indicate a substantial, statistically significant difference ($t = 2.26$, $p = 0.041$) in the perceived importance of community norms as a source of influence on officer discretion between levels of management. Top managers on average cited community norms as being 5.5 rings away from the bull's-eye of the discretionary target, while frontline officers suggested that community norms should be located 4.17 rings away from the bull's-eye of the target. As with political pressures, conventional wisdom may lead us to believe that differences of opinion, regarding this category, are to be expected. Here, one may argue that frontline officers have more interaction with community members in specific neighborhoods and are therefore more cognizant of community expectations and patterns of belief and behavior (Lipsky, 1980). From a normative standpoint, however, one can also identify three potential problems that such a discrepancy might create. First, officers at the street level may not be able to adequately justify or explain their discretionary choices if their managers are unacquainted with the norms of a specific zone. Second, because the bulk of their time may be consumed in dealing with the criminal subset of the population, frontline officers might overestimate their knowledge of community norms in general. Third, norms within each zone might vary. While some discretionary flexibility is called for to deal with this variation, firm lines must be drawn in the department's SOP manual to ensure some modicum of uniformity and consistency in officer behavior, no matter the beat (Meares, 2000).

Specific Organization Development Exercises

There are several methods which management can employ to ameliorate the disparity in the priority given to community norms between themselves and frontline officers.

First, management may conduct surveys, create focus groups, or hold town hall meetings so they can gain a deeper appreciation for and understanding of community concerns, and what is thought to be normal or appropriate citizen and officer behavior in their respective neighborhoods. This will also help frontline officers to correct any erroneous assumptions of community norms they have developed.

Second, managers may broaden their officers' experience (and prevent community capture, a phenomenon which occurs when officers begin trying to placate community members at the expense of performing their duties) by rotating officers one day each week to a precinct other than their usual precinct. This will help officers to communicate across beats and ascertain the city's general norms and needs.

Third, managers may ride along with subordinates so they can refamiliarize themselves with community norms.

Finally, managers might consider creating a community liaison system that serves to institutionalize attention to community norms.

Ideally, a specific position would be created within the organization where an officer would be dedicated to keeping his or her finger on the pulse of the community. Given widespread budgetary cutbacks, this might be unlikely. Still, regular officer-community meetings and events and officer training sessions are financially feasible and would serve many of the same purposes. When combined with the department's anonymous hotline and other outreach efforts (e.g., youth group), these efforts can help the agency develop stronger community bonds. In turn, the organization will be more successful in its attempts to demonstrate that it is part of the community, an increasingly important priority for public agencies (Boyes-Watson, 2006). The agency may also become better suited to cultivate the relationships necessary for the generation and use of information from the community (Bullock, 2010).

Overall Priority Level: Medium

Due to the distance between officer priorities and management priorities, this issue deserves prompt attention from managers. Because some departmental and community communication infrastructure is already in place, however, managers will find relative ease in planning and carrying out actions directed toward minimizing the gap between managers and line workers in this category.

Personal Values

Aggregate department responses show a large and highly statistically significant ($t = 2.41$, $p = 0.037$, two-tailed test) difference between the priority that managers and frontline officers give to their own personal values. Managers are apt to claim that the personal values category should be 4.2 rings away from the target's center. Frontline officers, on the other hand, claim that personal values ought to be listed only 1.86 rings from the center of the target. This category shows the greatest response distance between command staffers and frontline officers. Much of this disconnect may be rooted in what Maynard-Mooney and Musheno (2003) call the subject positions that officers occupy. Top managers may have already ingrained their respective subject positions into their agency's policies and rules. Frontline officers, however, have not had the opportunity to codify their values. Due to their relative inexperience compared to agency supervisors, they may in fact still be forming and cementing these values. From an optimistic standpoint, a discussion of personal values may offer two exciting opportunities for the department. First, awareness of a variety of subject positions and attendant values may help officers to develop an appreciation for the morals and values of their peers. This may help the department with diversity training and other efforts to share multiple perspectives on ethical concerns. Second, because they share a common commitment to law enforcement, officers are likely to be impressed with the commonality and compatibility of most of their values, despite their varying life experiences. In the spirit of standardizing officer response, managers should still address the importance of personal values compared to other discretionary considerations.

Specific Organization Development Exercises

Because officers' personal values are key components of their respective identities, this category requires a substantial amount of delicacy. The manager's challenge is to demonstrate respect and understanding for officers' personal values while helping frontline workers to understand the need for standardized, professional responses to each situation in which they find themselves. One may say the same about emotions and personal values, as is often said about fire: it can be one's greatest friend and one's worst enemy. To overcome the chasm between managers and frontline officers, a variety of tools are available.

For starters, managers may consider scenario-based training that asks respondents to judge the appropriate answer to each scenario and subsequently to explain how their personal values influenced their responses. Additionally, frontline officers can be asked to write personal mission and vision statements along with personal goals and measurable objectives. These officers can then be asked to explain the link between these personal aspirations and the overall department mission, vision, goals, and objectives. Frontline officers may be asked to read through the agency's policy manual and find support for their own personal values. This exercise may help officers to recognize that the policy manual and the agency's rules are not devoid of moral value, but much to the contrary, these rules are greatly informed by common personal values that almost all law enforcement officers share. Mentorship may also play a role in helping officers reconcile their personal values with organizational objectives (Dilworth, 1996; Henderson, 1985; Hunt & Michael, 1983; Sprafka & Kranda, 2010).

Overall Priority Level: Medium

The disconnect of the priority given to the personal values category between rank levels is the most pressing problem uncovered by this study and must be addressed in a timely fashion. The previously suggested exercises can be applied swiftly to address this concern.

Conclusion

Despite the three issue areas that merit attention and correction, this study provides evidence that the department has developed excellent communication infrastructure regarding most of the potential influences on discretion, especially those areas that managers consider most important (e.g., SOPs, legal liability, etc.). Furthermore, the impressive amount of agreement on all but three constraint categories suggests that the department can resolve the relatively minor issues presented in this study.

CASE THREE: THREE AGENCIES IN FORGOTTONIA

Single case studies from medium-sized cities in Illinois and Georgia provide preliminary evidence of the model's potential value. However, this will be the first study to apply the Target Model to data from multiple agencies in a single region, Forgottonia (a colloquial term for the West Central Illinois and East Central Iowa region). This study shows that the Target Model makes it possible to describe, analyze, and make initial generalizations regarding aggregate patterns of discretionary priorities between command staff and frontline officers in the region. This case involves three agencies. The population numbers for each city are 20,000; 25,464; and 40,366. In total, eighty respondents participated. Of the participants, twenty-three (29%) were command staff members and fifty-seven (71%) were frontline officers.

Results: Case Three (See Tables 10 and 11)

Remarkably, the results show that of the ten discretionary priorities (including the seldom used "other" option), managers and line workers only disagreed about the importance of two: community norms (t= -2.18, significant at the .032 p-level) and informal organizational values (t= 2.246, significant at the .028 p-level). I will briefly explain these differences beginning with informal organizational values.

Table 10: Frontline Officers' Response Ranks

Measure	Mean	Median
Agency Rules	2.18 (#1)	2.0
Legal Liability	3.25 (#3)	3.0
Personal Values	2.51 (#2)	2.0
Community Norms	3.72* (#4)	4.0
Informational Organizational Values	5.13* (#6)	5.0
Other Managers	4.86 (#5)	5.0
Professional Associations	6.94 (#8)	7.5
Political Pressure	6.55 (#7)	6.0
Accreditation Bodies	7.2 (#9)	8.0
Other	-	-

N= 57 *=p<.05

Table 11: Command Staff Members' Response Ranks

Measure	Mean	Median
Agency Rules	1.73 (#1)	2.0
Legal Liability	2.7 (#2)	3.0
Personal Values	3.1 (#4)	3.0
Community Norms	2.96* (#3)	3.0
Informational Organizational Values	6.23* (#6)	6.0
Other Managers	5.38 (#5)	6.0
Professional Associations	7.26 (#8)	7.0
Political Pressure	6.55 (#7)	6.5
Accreditation Bodies	7.55 (#9)	8.0
Other	-	-

N= 23 *=p<.05

BE THE CONSULTANT

Before reading the analysis section for this case study, put yourself in the shoes of the consultant/researcher. Given the two tables above, how would you:

1. Explain why there might be differences between rank levels?
2. Address the underlying causes of these differences?
3. Offer an action plan for managers and subordinates?

Find a partner and compare your strategies.

Discussion

Informal Organizational Norms

It should come as no surprise that frontline officers are better attuned to the informal organization made up of peer norms and values; this has been a tenet of basic organization theory for almost a century (Mayo, 1933; Roethlisberger & Dickson, 1939; Barnard, 1938). Managers most often have a predominant say in the rules, policies, processes, and structural arrangements that make up the formal organization. Line employees, on the other hand, rarely have a say in these facets of the formal organization but are charged with interpreting these SOPs into action at the street level (Mastrofski, 2004; Golembiewski, 1972; Gaines, 1978). Line employees thus develop their own peer norms and expectations (Argyris, 1962; Maynard-Mooney, Musheno, & Palumbo, 1990; Oberweis & Musheno, 1999). Adherence to these norms plays a determining role in whether one will be accepted by his or her peers or ostracized by them; as a result, the majority of line workers develop allegiance to these non-codified expectations (Reiser, 1974; Fyfe, 1996). This finding mirrors a similar discovery from a municipal police agency in Illinois (see Case One), and I refer the reader to this piece for specific organizational development exercises aimed at bringing about more agreement regarding this priority.

Community Norms

At first blush, the statistically significant difference in priority attributed to community norms seems a bit counterintuitive, especially if one stops to consider the negative direction of the sign. Conventional wisdom may lead us to believe that differences of opinion regarding this category are to be expected, albeit in the opposite direction. In theory, one may argue that frontline officers have more interaction with community members in specific neighborhoods and, therefore, are more cognizant of community expectations and patterns of belief and behavior (Argote, McEvily, & Reagans, 2003). However, command staff members have two advantages that might explain their collective awareness of community norms: experience in a given city and the trust of community members earned over a long time of service (Tyler & Huo, 2002).

Despite decreased visibility compared to that of the frontline officers, most managers have climbed through the ranks of these departments over a substantial period of time, helping them become more familiar with, and more apt to consider, the values and expectations of the community. In addition, these values and expectations are likely to be communicated to top managers by city managers, mayors, and councils who have also served in municipal government for long periods. These values may also be communicated by local citizen groups and by individual citizens who reside in the department's jurisdiction (Denhardt & Denhardt, 2003). This line of logic assumes that experience rather than rank is the variable that best explains the differences between command staffers and frontline officers. If this is the case, the most appropriate recommendation for eliminating this discrepancy might be for the command staff members to patiently wait while their departments' junior officers gain more experience in dealing with this specific community.

Unfortunately, such a passive solution simply takes too much time to address what some consider a critical area of intradepartmental communication and decision-making. In the following section, I offer more immediate and concrete suggestions for improving communication related to the influence that community norms should have on officers' use of discretion.

Conclusion

The three presented case studies demonstrate the value of the Target Model as a tool for analyzing single agency data as well as aggregate data from multiple agencies. This study also shows that the Target Model can help researchers and practitioners understand patterns and generalize about discretionary priorities in a given agency or region. I urge researchers to replicate this study in other regions and at larger units of analysis (e.g., state level), so we may continue to evaluate the Target Model's efficacy in highlighting and resolving communication differences between rank levels. The next step in this line of research, of course, is a test of the Target Model at the state and national levels to determine its utility for making even greater generalizations. The following chapter will highlight one of the first attempts to do this, with survey data from over 100 sheriffs in three states.

OPPORTUNITY FOR REFLECTION

Personal Values, Community Norms, Political Pressures

Personal Values

Consider that managers in this study were less likely to give priority to their personal values when making discretionary choices. Could it be that the personal values of management are reflected in the official departmental policies that managers create? What are some ways in which the process of creating SOPs for agencies could reflect officers' personal values?

What are some personal values that you have trouble reconciling with your current or future career in policing? Do you have a plan for addressing these concerns?

Can you think of any biases you hold? That is, do you tend to understand or empathize with certain types of people more easily than others? What are some strategies you could use to better understand or empathize with others?

Community Norms

What are some possible explanations for the different priority levels we see with the community norms variable? Could it be that frontline officers are more often exposed to members of the community in the course of their daily patrols?

How did you become familiar with the norms of your community? If this seems too abstract, think all the way back to the first community to which you belonged. For instance, how did you become aware of the norms and expectations of your family?

Can you think of other strategies for engaging command staff members with the community more frequently?

Political Pressures
Is policing insulated from politics? Should it be?

In your opinion, is it appropriate for top managers to be more aware of political pressures than their subordinates?

Why would managers want their subordinates to pay attention to local politics and the demands of political officials and groups in their respective communities?

What do you know about local politics? What are some ways that you participate in local politics? How do you get your information? If you wanted to become more aware of local politics, what could you do as an individual?

Chapter 4

Do as I Say! Or, Do as I Say, Not as I Have Done! Self-Reported Accountability Priorities for County Sheriffs and Their Subordinates

Student Learning Outcomes	Practical Learning Outcomes
Students will be able to compare and contrast case study application of the Target Model to aggregate survey-based approaches and comment on the relative advantages and disadvantages of each.	Practitioners will be able to compare and contrast case study application of the Target Model to aggregate survey-based approaches.
Students will be able to describe some unique characteristics of the county sheriff's office when compared to the municipal police department.	Practitioners will be able to describe these same characteristics.
Students will discuss accountability as an aggregate phenomenon as well as a department-specific consideration.	Practitioners will be able to evaluate trends in sheriffs' responses and compare them to their own views of top managers' priorities.

An earlier version of this article appeared in the *Law Enforcement Executive Forum*, 12(1), pp. 96-104

INTRODUCTION

Organization theory is filled with literature examining motivation as the crucial variable managers must manipulate in order to receive acceptable levels of productivity from subordinates (Organ, 1988; McKnight, Cummings, & Chervany, 1998; Veiga, 1988). Typically, management literature emphasizes the need for supervisors to communicate their priorities to their workers (Suchman, 1995, p. 586). An added complexity within this relationship is the fact that some managers have different expectations for themselves than they do for those under their supervision (Whetten, 1978, p. 255). This paper examines this phenomenon through the eyes of county sheriffs in three U.S. states: Missouri, North Carolina, and Nebraska. We will begin by explaining why the county sheriff, an important public manager, is an excellent subject for this type of inquiry. We will then review pertinent management literature from which we drew our hypotheses. Next, we will present two competing hypotheses regarding the relationship between a manager's self-reported priorities and those which the manager reports for subordinates. Afterward, we will empirically test these hypotheses using a series of linear regression models. Finally, we will discuss our findings and suggest how future research can build upon our study.

THE PECULIAR MANAGEMENT ROLE OF THE COUNTY SHERIFF

Holding the office of county sheriff brings about a series of distinct roles, responsibilities, and accountability considerations (Falcone & Wells, 1995; LaFrance & Placide, 2010a). The sheriff serves as the head of an organization (the sheriff's office) that engages in a range of activities including, but certainly not limited to, running the county jail, providing law enforcement services for county residents, staffing courts with bailiffs and security officials, and serving warrants and civil papers (Falcone & Wells, 1995). Furthermore, the sheriff is most often elected to the position. As a result, the sheriff not only has to juggle effective service provision in several realms but also must be mindful of the electorate and the decisions and opinions of peer-elected officials (LaFrance & Placide, 2010a). In such an instance, a complication arises. Namely, the democratically elected sheriff is charged with commanding sworn and non-sworn personnel who, for the most part, were selected based on merit criteria (LaFrance & Placide, 2010b). Thus, one may reasonably suspect that political pressures resonate more with the sheriff than it does with their subordinates. Additionally, the nature of the sheriff's office forces the sheriff to span the boundaries of several organizations and systems of service provision (public, private, and nonprofit) and governance (in terms of federal-state-local relationships and functional dimensions). Therefore, the sheriff might be more apt to consider the opinions of managers outside of the organization when making decisions. Does this mean the sheriff would expect officers to mimic his or her decision calculus or, instead, to limit themselves to intra-agency rules and considerations? We simply cannot say with any certainty. These dynamics lead us to construct two broad, oppositional hypotheses.

HYPOTHESIS I: MANAGERS EXPECTS SUBORDINATES TO MIRROR THEIR PRIORITIES

Hypothesis I asserts that sheriffs expect subordinates to mirror their respective priorities. This hypothesis makes intuitive sense, as sheriffs can foster coherent and consistent communication throughout the organization if they insist that their subordinates think as they do. An additional benefit of this logic is that sheriffs may be more apt to manage fairly if their performance evaluation criteria for the officers whom they oversee are congruent with the evaluation criteria they set for themselves. Finally, this arrangement has the potential to offer a built-in accountability mechanism (and sets a foundation for a relationship premised on trust) in the often studied manager-subordinate relationship.

One relevant piece of literature points to the results of managers and subordinates seeing eye-to-eye. Management scholar Bruce Kemelgor (1982, p.158) explains that "[a] supervisor should value his subordinates to the degree that they help to attain the supervisor's work goals, and he will be more attracted to those who share a similarity in basic attitudes and values." In addition, Kemelgor (1982) claims that his study "suggests that value similarities could function to lessen conflict, improve communication, and cooperation. There is also possibly an increase in conformity and morale" (p.158).

Despite the aforementioned merits of this approach, it may be quite naïve to expect workers occupying completely different roles to think alike. If taken to an extreme, this type of interaction can actually be dangerous in that it forgoes contextual considerations that are tied to each rank level and role within the organization. Furthermore, too much consensus can lead to the problem of groupthink where no team member wishes to point out flaws in decisions made by the leaders of an organization for fear of ostracism from his or her work group (Janis, 1982).

HYPOTHESIS II: MANAGERS EXPECTS SUBORDINATES TO HAVE DIFFERENT PRIORITIES THAN THEIRS

Hypothesis II is premised on the notion that contextual considerations of each rank level are ultimately more important to the top manager of an agency than uniformity of values and standardization of priorities. Thompson's (1967) description of the manager's role in buffering the technical core is closely linked to this phenomenon. This buffering role prevents the core workers of an agency from experiencing distress or confusion that could result from environmental shocks, enabling the core workers instead to focus on the technical precision that is expected in their specialized organizational subunits. This, too, could be considered a good management practice as it would be likely to minimize the stress to which a sheriff's officers are exposed. This is an especially important consideration given the general high-risk nature of law enforcement careers. However, as foreshadowed in the presentation of Hypothesis I, this approach to management may have drawbacks in terms of the consistency of expectations and the fairness of performance evaluations.

Having presented each hypothesis, we now endeavor to test them in order to determine which hypothesis is a more accurate description of the sheriff's approach to management decision-making.

METHOD AND PROCEDURES

The Target Model of Discretion was developed to understand the priority level officer's ascribe nine different categories: Legal Liabilities, Community Norms, SOPs, Political Pressures, Personal Values, Other Managers, Professional Associations, Accreditation Bodies, and Informal Organizations. We then used this model to formulate a survey to send to sheriffs to test the above hypotheses. Participants were asked to prioritize ten items based on the nine categories listed above from their perspective as managers. Another question on the survey asked: "When thinking about how your officers make discretionary choices, in what order [would] you prefer they prioritize the following?"

We then sent this survey to all the sheriffs in Missouri, Nebraska, and North Carolina. From the 308 sheriffs in these three states, we received 107 responses (response rate = 34.7%). For each sheriff, we sent three mailings: an introduction, the survey, and a reminder. There is no reason to expect any systematic response bias since the response rate was not extremely low and the lack of responses has no reason to be correlated with the variables in our model. After receiving the survey responses, we analyzed the results using Ordinary Least Squares (OLS) regression. This statistical technique is a way of approximating a linear relationship between a dependent variable and several independent variables in order to predict the value of a dependent variable based on changes in the independent variable. It is very similar to the Slope-Intercept one learns in algebra. For more information, see Michael Lewis-Beck's *Applied Regression: An Introduction* (1980).

FINDINGS

The results for the first nine models are shown below in Table 12. According to these results, a manager's own priority level on each discretion category explains between 44-80% of the variance in the priority level the manager wants his or her employees to place on each category. Compelling research suggests that on seven of the nine categories of priorities, the priority that the manager places on each category alone explains over half of the variation in the priority he or she wants employees to place on that category.

Table 12: Nine OLS Regression Models: Priority Level of Manager Regressed on Priority Level Expected of Employee[1]

Categories	Constant	Coefficient	R Square
Legal Liability	0.469 (0.157)	0.79 (0.068)	0.565
Community Norms	1.129 (0.309)	0.743 (0.067)	0.554
SOPs	0.325 (0.162)	0.75 (0.054)	0.657
Political Pressures	1.736 (0.493)	0.782 (0.063)	0.617
Personal Values	1.247 (0.218)	0.693 (0.061)	0.564
Other Managers	1.215 (0.56)	0.785 (0.089)	0.447
Professional Associations	1.744 (0.387)	0.765 (0.057)	0.656
Accreditation Bodies	0.547 (0.375)	0.915 (0.048)	0.794
Informal Organizations	1.86 (0.468)	0.722 (0.076)	0.484

---

1 The categories listed are the nine independent variables used in understanding the manager's expectations of employees. We can compare the relative importance of each of these variables by examining the value of each variable's R-squared value. The closer the R-squared value reaches 1, the better fit the variable is in determining what is expected of employees. Standard errors in parentheses.

We then constructed graphs to show how a manager's placement of the category's priority level affects the priority level he or she wants employees to also place on that category. The matching line provides a reference point. This shows how the line would look if the manager consistently wanted employees to place the same priority level on a category that he or she placed on that category. When the regression line is below the matching line, it means the manager wanted employees to place a higher priority level on the category than he or she did. When the regression line is above the matching line, the manager wanted officers to place a lower priority on that category than he or she did.

On Legal Liabilities and SOPs, managers almost always wanted their employees to place a higher priority than they did. On Political Pressures, Professional Associations, and Informal Organizations, managers almost always wanted their employees to place a lower priority than they did.

There was mixed evidence about Community Norms, Personal Values, and the referential actions of other managers. Sheriffs who placed a higher priority on these values wanted their officers to place a lower value and vice versa. Finally, managers on average almost always wanted their employees to match their priority level on Accreditation Bodies.

These results provide support for both hypotheses and show that the managers' expectation of their employees' priorities depends on the particular category of influence. For example, it makes sense that managers want their employees to have a higher priority on the rules (Legal Liabilities and SOPs) and may see themselves as having more discretion from the rules. Considering that some categories of influence are outside the managers' realm of control, it is reasonable to see why managers may want their officers to place a lower priority on categories, which are outside the realm of the managers' control such as Political Pressures, Professional Associations, and Informal Organizations.

The conflicting results about Community Norms, Personal Values, and Other Managers do not support either hypothesis. More research is needed to see what influences managers' views of these categories. The level of priority placed on Accreditation Bodies expected to be shared by managers and employees likely results from the accreditation bodies' effects on the organization as a whole.

CONCLUSION

We have evaluated two rival hypotheses regarding the degree of emulation sheriffs wish to see from their subordinate officers when it comes to the ranking of discretionary priorities. Findings reveal support for each rival hypothesis when looking at specific categories of discretionary influence. In essence, the veracity of either hypothesis is contingent on the discretionary influence category under investigation. As a result, one may surmise that the validity of each hypothesis is contingent upon the role expectations inherent in the managers' and subordinates' roles. We have also encountered categories wherein the relationships were not straightforward enough to allow us to draw conclusions. Taken as a whole, our results are more provocative than conclusive. From a scientific standpoint, this outcome is a bit disappointing. From a practical standpoint, however, our findings serve to illuminate the awesome complexity inherent in managing a public enterprise. Future research should aim to provide more definitive answers to the presented puzzles while being mindful of the numerous and daunting expectations to which public managers are held.

Graph 1: Priority Level of Legal Liabilities

Graph 2: Priority Level of Community Norms

Graph 3: Priority Level of Standard Operating Procedures

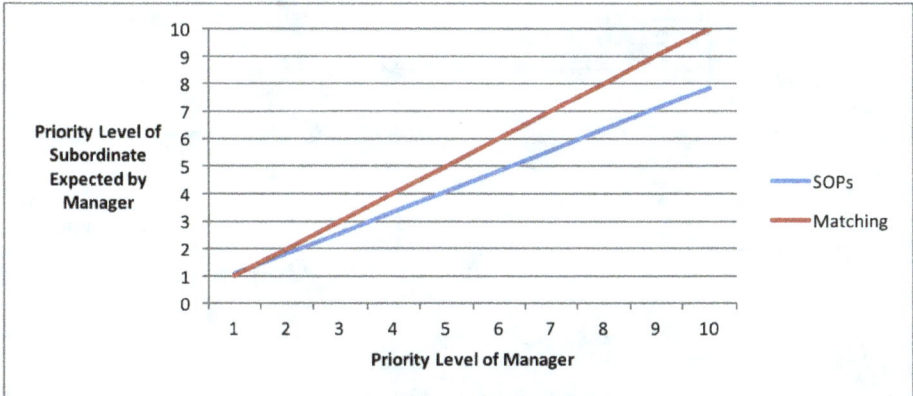

Graph 4: Priority Level of Political Pressures

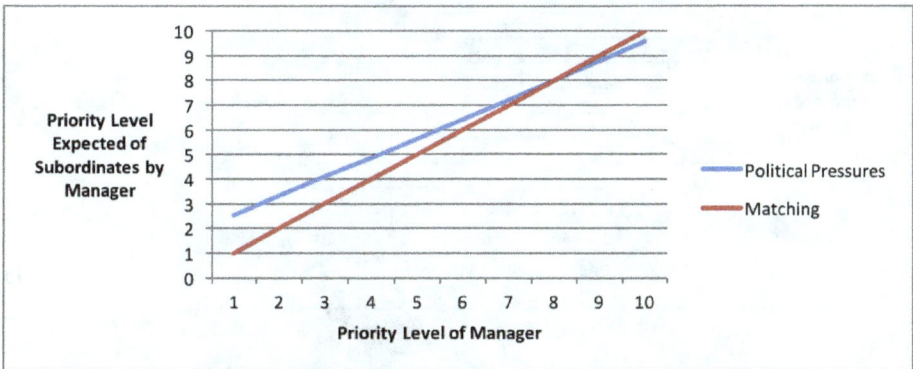

Graph 5: Priority Level of Personal Values

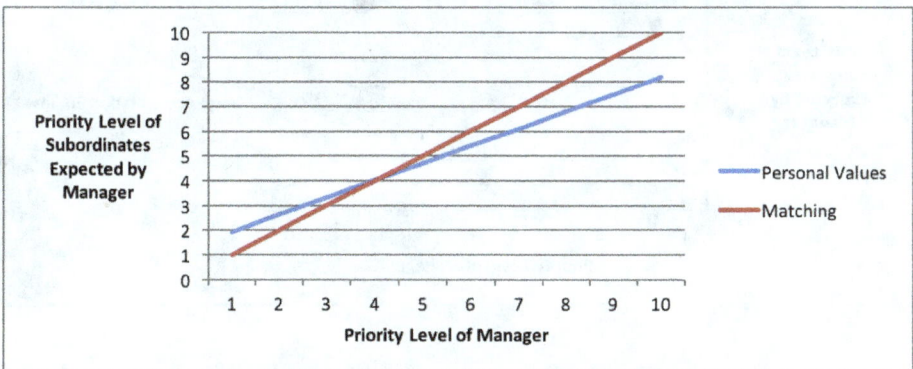

Graph 6: Priority Level of Other Managers

Priority Level of Subordinate Expected by Manager (y-axis)

Priority Level of Manager (x-axis)

— Other Managers
— Matching

Graph 7: Priority Level of Professional Associations

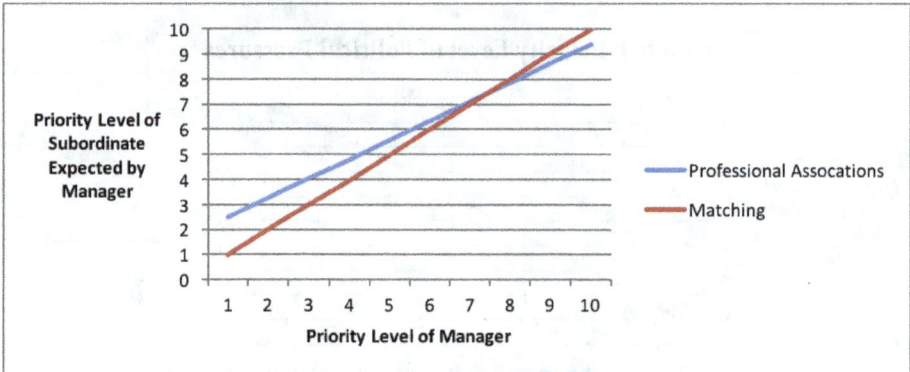

Priority Level of Subordinate Expected by Manager (y-axis)

Priority Level of Manager (x-axis)

— Professional Assocations
— Matching

Graph 8: Priority Level of Accreditation Bodies

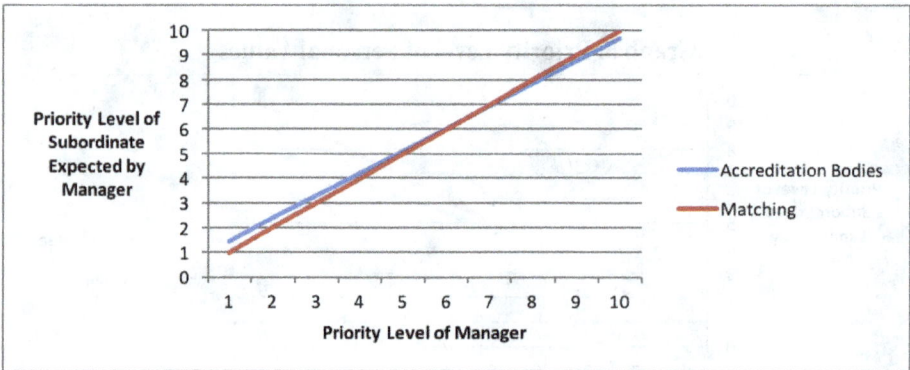

Priority Level of Subordinate Expected by Manager (y-axis)

Priority Level of Manager (x-axis)

— Accreditation Bodies
— Matching

Graph 9: Priority Level of Informal Organizations

Part III

Chapter 5

Using the Target Model of Discretion to Evaluate Intra-Agency Communication: A Guide for Managers and Scholars

Student Learning Outcomes	Practical Learning Outcomes
Students will be able to develop a target survey and discuss the process of using it to collect data.	Practitioners will be able to develop a survey and discuss the process of administering it to collect data in their agencies.
Students will be able to describe the process of analyzing data using a simple t-test.	Practitioners will be able to describe the process of analyzing data using a simple t-test.
Students will be able to discuss how the data analysis can be used to provide suggestions for organization development.	Practitioners will be able to recognize some likely implications for organization development that arise from data analyses.
Students will be able to describe the strengths and weaknesses of the Target Model's approach.	Practitioners will be able to do the same, while also articulating why a command staff member or a frontline officer would be interested in using the Target Model.

An earlier version of this essay appeared in *The Legal and Economic Aspects of Public Administration in the Russian Federation and the USA: Theory, Practice, and Research*, pp. 318-324.

INTRODUCTION

Many law enforcement managers and scholars want to assess communication patterns in individual police agencies. Until recently this task required a great deal of time and resources. Fortunately, the Target Model of Discretion makes such an assessment very quick and inexpensive. In this brief essay, we will explain the step-by-step process of using the Target Model to assess organizational communication regarding the appropriate use of discretion by officers in a given agency. After reading this guide, managers and scholars will be able to replicate the work we have done in evaluating organizational communication, and they will be able to contribute to the minimization of communication gaps between frontline officers and their managers.

STEP ONE: DETERMINE YOUR RATIONALE FOR ASSESSING COMMUNICATION

As a scholar, your rationale behind considering police discretion is most likely research. As a manager, however, you may have several reasons for wanting to assess communication. In the worst case scenario, a manager may feel as if his or her agency is unable to effectively communicate; the use of an assessment tool may be critical to prevent disasters related to communication failures. A manager alternatively, may be seeking to improve already successful communication patterns. Research shows that many agencies will fall somewhere between these two extremes (LaFrance, 2010). A typical manager is likely to find acceptable or excellent levels of agreement on many discretionary priorities and some areas in which communication can be improved. Regardless of the manager's rationale for choosing to conduct or participate in this assessment, the manager must recognize that doing so may expose any of the agency's hidden issues. Frankly, this tool forces managers to recognize shortcomings in their organizational communication patterns. If the manager is unwilling to acknowledge that his or her agency is flawed in some ways, the assessment will be a waste of the time and effort for all involved. If, however, the manager is willing to suffer a temporarily bruised ego, he or she will likely be rewarded with enhanced organizational communication in the agency.

STEP 2: SHARE YOUR INTENTIONS WITH MEMBERS OF YOUR DEPARTMENT, EMPHASIZE ANONYMITY, AND PUBLICIZE THE DISTRIBUTION AND COLLECTION DATE

After you have evaluated your intentions for conducting this analysis, share them with all members of the agency. This will be a chance for you to emphasize the importance of the project to the agency as a whole and to encourage participation. Here, the manager or scholar may emphasize that he or she is only looking for aggregate patterns in responses and is not seeking to single out any member of the agency for retribution. The manager will later reinforce the anonymity of the exercise by asking officers to detach consent and participation forms from their completed surveys and turn each in separately. It is wise to publicize the exercise two or more weeks in advance so each agency member is aware of the date of survey distribution and collection.

Step 3: Distribute the Blank Target and Survey Form (See Appendix B)

Command staff members and frontline officers will be given variants of the same question. Frontline officers will be asked, "Keeping how you use discretion as an officer in mind, how would you rank the importance of each of the following as boundaries on discretion?" Command staff members will be asked, "When thinking of how you would like for your officers to use discretion, how would you rank the importance of each of the following as boundaries on discretion?"

Step 4: Collect the Completed Surveys Anonymously

Assign a trusted officer with the task of collecting completed surveys. Task this person with ensuring that each respondent indicated whether he or she is a frontline officer or command staff member. Other than this distinction, information that could identify a respondent should be omitted.

Step 5: Make a Spreadsheet and Enter Responses by Discretionary Category for Each Rank Level; Conduct an Independent Samples t-test

Open a blank Excel worksheet. Enter responses by category (e.g., community norms, legal liability, etc.), into two columns, one for frontline officers and one for command staff members' responses. Using the sum feature in Excel ($\sum$) add up the number of target rings that members of each group ascribed to this category. Next take the arithmetical average (mean) from each group by dividing the total number by the number of respondents in each group. Then take the standard deviation (STDev) of each group. (For a thorough explanation of the process by which the standard deviation is calculated, you may visit a website that offers free tutorials, such as www.stattrek.com). Once you have the average for each group and the standard deviation, you will conduct an independent samples *t*-test, a relatively simple statistical procedure.

To conduct the *t*-test, you will select "T.TEST" from the "statistical functions" menu in Excel and select the option for a two-tailed test. More detailed instructions for conducting the *t*-test are available online, at sites such as http://depts.alverno.edu/nsmt/stats.htm. It may be preferable to contact a social sciences professor for assistance with running this statistical analysis. Once you have found the *t* value (the between groups difference), you can check the "critical values for *t*" table online at: http://www.statsoft.com/textbook/distribution-tables/#t. You will need to calculate the degrees of freedom for the test (the number of total respondents, minus two). Once you know how many degrees of freedom you have, simply match this to your *t* value to know if the result is statistically significant (i.e., the results were not derived by mere chance). You may set your threshold for significance at .10 (10 chances in 100 that your results are derived by chance alone) or .05 (5 chances in 100 that your results are derived by chance alone). Each category that yields a statistically significant between-groups difference (i.e., a significant *t* score) is a category that you should examine in the subsequent step.

STEP 6: CONSIDER THE RESULTS AND TAKE ACTION ACCORDINGLY

At this point, the manager or scholar will have put a great deal of work into the assessment. You should take a few moments to evaluate the results and their implications for the agency being studied. While we tend to focus on statistically significant differences (areas for improvement), it is also wise to consider the categories of discretionary influence in which no significant differences were found. The lack of statistical differences in response categories between groups is a powerful indication that agency managers are investing tremendous effort in communicating discretionary priorities to frontline officers, and these efforts have been successful. In fact, if no significant differences are recorded between response groups, you should consider planning an event to congratulate all members of the agency on the health of their communication patterns. You may also hold an open discussion focused on the best methods by which these communication patterns can continue to yield success.

If categories of discretionary influence are in need of attention, you and your agency should study these differences and consider underlying causes. You may find it helpful to discuss these issues with other members of the agency's command staff and, eventually, the frontline officers. If a scholar is not involved in the project, this may be an opportunity for you to ask for some guidance from an organization theorist or organization development expert. Scholarly guidance, though not entirely necessary, may be beneficial in helping managers to understand root causes in categorical differences between rank levels. Once root causes have been identified, you must create an action plan to arrest them.

STEP 7: CREATING AND IMPLEMENTING AN ACTION PLAN

The scholar or manager involved in the administration of the survey and analysis of the results has an obligation to move beyond diagnosis and offer some suggestions for treating the communication maladies that this process uncovers. While this may seem to be an incredibly daunting task, you can simplify matters by revisiting the original purpose of the process. All categories challenged by discretionary constraint can be improved by communication between rank levels. If you want to know why officers have different priorities, you should visit with each of them and spend some time outside of the office and in their environment. Afterwards, it is likely that you will be in a better position to choose tools and make decisions aimed at reconciling discretionary priorities. These decisions will become part of a larger strategic plan for enhancing organizational communication with agreed upon goals and measurable objectives.

STEP 8: SEEKING FEEDBACK AND RE-TESTING

After implementing the plan, you and your agency should evaluate the progress made toward the achievement of each goal. You should seek feedback from all members of the organization related to this action plan and make the adjustments as necessary. After three to four months, re-test all agency members to see if the communication flaws have been resolved in the agency. If not, reconsider the process of strategic planning.

A CAVEAT TO THIS PROCESS

Priorities will not align perfectly between rank levels in a police agency. In fact, these organizations are most often structured to ensure that managers and subordinates deal with differing types of influences and concerns (Thompson, 1967). The inability to reach perfection should not preclude efforts to advance understanding between frontline officers and their command staff members. Even if managers and officers do not always agree on priorities, this exercise can help members of each group to understand and respect the reasons behind divergent decisions. Just because an officer or manager failed to choose a given priority in making a choice, he or she might be able to pinpoint other considerations that took precedence in his or her mind.

Chapter 6

Hands-on Tools for Discussion, Team Building, and Planning

This chapter is full of practical tools that will assist managers, officers, students, and instructors to discuss officer discretion. Additionally, I have supplied tools that may be used in team-building exercises in the academy, squad room, or classroom. Finally, I have provided a rudimentary strategic planning guide to help managers and their officers to identify their organization's future goals.

HANDS-ON TOOL A:

PRACTICAL EXPLANATION OF THE TARGET MODEL'S DISCRETIONARY PRIORITIES

While the previous section shows how scholars list and describe the priorities an officer or manager tends to use in making discretionary choices, this section is intended to provide some concrete definitions to clarify the meaning of the various influences.

Community Norms

Each city, town, and county has its own expectations regarding the roles and purposes of policing and how officers should make decisions that reflect the communities they serve. Consider this example from the small town of Harvard, Illinois. Each year, the quaint dairy town celebrates Milk Days. Milk Days are marked by a weekend of festivities, including a carnival. The biggest celebration occurs on Saturday when an impressive two to three hour parade marches through the heart of the town. A considerable amount of adults drink beer, or other alcoholic beverages, and visit with their neighbors, going from bar to bar or house to house. Therefore, the city temporarily suspends the enforcement of open container laws for pedestrians for the length of the parade. Fining or detaining someone for possessing an open container of alcohol would violate the community's norms.

Personal Values

The Personal Values category is meant to capture the idea of personally set individual morals. Here, you may consider your own religious or spiritual values as an example. These values may not always line up with what is considered to be legal or illegal. Moreover, these values may increase your awareness of certain activities or groups. They may even encourage you to empathize with those whom you know share your values or life experiences. One of the biggest challenges officers face is striking a balance between these personal values and the professional role they occupy.

Legal Liability

Society is becoming increasingly litigious. From day one on the job, officers will be threatened with lawsuits. While most of these are empty threats, some are very real and can have damaging effects on one's career and personal life. This external threat can make officers cautious when fulfilling their duties. The threat of lawsuits and changes in case law can force an agency to rewrite policies or revise practices.

Professional Associations

Professional associations at the local, state, national, and international levels will sometimes dictate standards for behavior or suggest practices for dealing with a variety of law enforcement scenarios. The associations provide valuable information, training, conferences, and other benefits. They can limit autonomy for an agency by endorsing or discouraging certain decisions ranging from the type of tee shirt officers may wear under their uniforms to how traffic stops are conducted.

Accreditation Bodies

To many in law enforcement, accreditation bodies offer the gold seal of quality assurance in an agency's practices. Other managers and officers might see accreditation as nothing more than a bumper sticker or a bragging point. Regardless of an individual's perspective, the accreditation process often brings a set of model policies to an agency. Action outside of these model policies is limited, though some situations do not conform to their "one size fits all" nature.

Standard Operating Procedures (SOPs)

SOPs are designed to standardize behavior among members of a work unit. These policies are written so that officers will know what agency expectations are in a given situation. SOPs are helpful in providing guidance for officers in decision making, especially when command staff members are not immediately available for consultation. Though they address a wide variety of situations, these rules are not perfect and create the need for some degree of interpretation and application on the part of the officer.

Other Managers

Law enforcement often requires coordination and cooperation with other agencies. Sometimes, managers outside of one's own agency might suggest, encourage, or even demand that officers use certain decision criteria. This is especially true with close or overlapping jurisdictions, or with decisions involving multiple levels of government such as the Department of Homeland Security's recent order that all radio transmissions be made in "plain speech" rather than "10 codes." Interacting with other managers can aid in the creation of logical plans to deal with law enforcement scenarios spanning more than one jurisdiction (geographical or governmental). A certain degree of sovereignty is relinquished upon entering into these agreements or deciding to follow the dictates of other managers.

Peer Influences and the Informal Organization

Informal organization refers to the unwritten, and sometimes unspoken, way in which an agency operates at its core. People may speak of the informal organization as "how things are done around here." To understand these informal expectations an officer has to experience them. For instance, some officers consider themselves to be in positions of authority even if they are of the same rank as their peers. Some traditions are never written into the agency's SOP manual. Instead, some behaviors are informally incentivized while other behaviors are discouraged by peers in an organization. The informal organization is where one learns how the agency really operates. Sometimes, the informal organization can be quite different from the formal organization that is characterized by written standards, stated goals, and objectives.

Political Pressures

Political Pressures are important sources of external control over an agency's behavior, and they come in two distinct forms: direct and indirect. Direct political pressure often comes from elected officials or appointed administrators who communicate their desires in public and private meetings. Managers and officers must be attuned to these desires since their elected (e.g., city or county council members) and appointed (e.g., city or county managers) overseers will no doubt be plugged into political concerns. This is essential because the elected and appointed overseers often expect attention to these desires and these desires often generate accompanying political support. Indirect political pressures come from individual community members or community groups. Many community groups express their desires and threaten certain actions if these desires are unmet. For instance, some chapters of Mothers Against Drunk Driving (M.A.D.D.) call for enhanced enforcement of drunken driving laws. If members believe that enforcement of these laws is insufficient, they may complain to law enforcement administrators, city managers, mayors, or council members. This category is especially tricky for elected county sheriffs, as these groups can provide and influence votes in a given election cycle.

HANDS-ON TOOL B

Teambuilding: Organization and Environment Assessment

Before comparing and contrasting discretionary priorities within your agency, take a moment to consider each of the following categories. You will be provided with a list of discussion questions within each category. You may begin by writing out your thoughts in response to the questions in each category. Afterward, you can compare your responses with a partner or a small group. Remember, there are no correct or incorrect responses.

Personal Values

What are some of the most important values or beliefs you hold?

Where did you learn these values? For example, did you read a certain religious or ethical text? Did these values come from important family members, mentors, or friends?

Consider your personal demographic characteristics (e.g., age, race, etc.). How have these characteristics influenced your personal values?

Consider your life experiences (e.g., education, previous jobs, relationships, etc.). How have these experiences influenced your personal values? Which events, if any, have caused you to rethink these values or other deeply held beliefs?

Have you ever experienced a moment when your personal values conflicted with your professional role and obligations? What did you do? How did you learn from it?

Political Pressures

Describe the political structure of your service jurisdiction (e.g., city, county, etc.). Is there a professional city or county administrator? How many members serve on the legislative body? Is there an elected executive (e.g., mayor, commission chair)? Have there been any changes in this political structure in recent years?

What are some important powers held by elected or appointed officials outside your agency (e.g., setting the budget, hiring, creating ordinances for you to enforce, etc.)?

What are some important powers your agency holds in relation to the political structure?

What is your overall impression of the demands or requests made by members of the political structure overseeing your agency? Are the demands or requests reasonable? Why or why not?

Can you recall a situation in which your agency had to change its policies or typical decisions in light of political pressures? What happened?

Which citizen groups are most active in local politics? Do they make any particular demands (e.g., M.A.D.D. might want enhanced D.W.I./D.U.I. enforcement)? What does your agency do in response to these demands? Does your agency deal directly with these groups, or is it more common for the groups to meet with local political officials first?

Informal Organization Norms

Describe your agency's inner-work environment. Is it collegial, competitive, hostile, enjoyable, or some mix of these characteristics, and/or others? Which practices or people contribute to this environment?

Are there any members of your agency who command attention or respect for some reason other than their rank? What about these members is it that earns them this respect or attention?

Within the workplace, does your agency observe or practice any traditions or rituals that are not part of agency rules or orders? For instance, some agencies have a tradition of expecting the next shift to arrive 15 minutes or so prior to beginning work so they can briefly be informed of important occurrences from the past few hours.

Outside of the workplace, are there traditions or rituals that are common? For instance, some coworkers may organize a weekly poker game or an occasional visit to a restaurant or bar. Are there any informal events hosted by your agency's command staff (e.g., picnics, an officers' ball, etc.)?

What are some things a person would never know about the inner dynamics of your agency without working there?

How often do you interact with members of the command staff? How often do you interact with the chief executive?

To what extent are command staff members "plugged in" to the informal organization? Do they participate in the informal traditions or rituals you have described? Do they know you as a person or just as a badge number?

Community Norms

Think about the community you serve. What are some important features of your community's demographic makeup? Have there been any note-worthy changes in the demographics of your community in recent years? What are some events, or points of cultural or historical significance, for the community?

How much do you know about the community's history? Can you think of any crucial events in the community's history that might have influenced the community (e.g., the community was/was not chosen as a site for a university or factory)?

What are some of the community's top priorities? How do you know these?

Are there any major divisions within the community? What causes/caused these divisions? How does your agency deal with them?

Are there any divisions between your agency and the community it serves? How did these develop? How can your agency begin to work on these divisions?

Describe some opportunities citizens have to interact with frontline officers, command staff members, or both in your agency (other than being processed as offenders). Can your agency do something to enhance these opportunities?

How much does a typical community member know about your agency? If they are curious, how can they obtain more information (e.g., through a website, a community service officer, etc.)?

What are some of your community's top law enforcement concerns (e.g., burglaries, speeding, noise violations)? Are there any areas of law enforcement that the community seems to want to see enhanced or reduced?

Professional Associations

Of which, if any, professional associations (international, national, state, local) are you a member?

Why did you become a member?

What do you do for the professional association (e.g., pay dues, serve on committees, etc.)?

What does the professional association do for you?

Generally speaking, what are some things that professional associations do for your agency?

What are some mandates, suggestions, or "best practices" that professional associations encourage you or your agency to follow?

Accreditation Bodies

Is your agency accredited? If so, by which accreditation body (e.g., CALEA, etc.)?

How does (or would) accreditation affect the day to day work of your agency?

How does (or would) accreditation affect the overall goals or mission of your agency?

What are some advantages of accreditation?

What are some disadvantages of accreditation?

Reflecting on these advantages and disadvantages, do you think your agency *should* or *should not* be accredited?

Standard Operating Procedures

Does your agency have a set of Standard Operating Procedures (SOPs)?

How familiar are you with your agency's policy manual?

What are some ways in which you become familiar with your agency's policy manual (e.g., training, roll call quizzes, etc.)?

How thorough is the SOP manual?

How helpful is the SOP in making decisions?

How are changes (additions, revisions, deletions) to the SOP decided?

How much voice do you have in determining agency rules and policies?

What are some ways in which command staff members can solicit input regarding changes in agency rules and policies?

Do you pay more, less, or about the same attention to SOPs now as you did when first began working with this agency?

What is missing from your SOP manual that you would like to see?

Is there anything you would like to see removed from the SOPs?

Legal Liability Concerns

What are some of your biggest concerns regarding legal liability in your profession?

Were you ever named in a suit related to your professional role? What was the outcome?

How well do frontline officers and command staff members prevent potential legal liabilities?

How is information obtained and communicated regarding changes in case law that may affect your agency? Can these processes be improved?

How often are SOPs revised to reflect legal liability concerns or changes in case law?

What are some strategies your agency can use to reduce legal liability risks?

How much influence do external legal actors (judges, lawyers, potentially litigious groups) have on the overall goals and mission of your agency?

How much influence do external legal actors have on day to day operations in your agency?

Other Managers

Consider all of the interactions you and others within your agency have with other local, state, federal, private, or non-profit agencies. (It may help to diagram/draw some of these interactions).

How much influence do your agency's command staff members have on the decisions or policies of these other agencies?

How much influence do these other agencies' managers have on your agency?

Are there opportunities for partnerships or cooperation between your agency and another agency? What are these opportunities? How can they be fulfilled?

Are there areas of your agency's operations which are too heavily influenced by other agencies, their respective command staff members, or both? If this is the case, what can be done?

HANDS-ON TOOL C

Scenarios to Initiate Discussion of Target Model Priorities

Informal Organization Scenarios

A Hairy Situation

While the department's SOP manual explicitly calls for neatly groomed facial hair, several third shift officers have bet on who can grow the largest beard for a contest sponsored by a popular waterfowl-based television show. The contest will last for one month at the end of which a winner will be declared. What action, if any, should the shift supervisor take?

Paying Dues?

Officer Bruce just began his law enforcement career two weeks ago. The FTO assigned to him, Officer Waddell, made it clear that Officer Bruce must perform extra favors for him at the end of each shift. Last week, Officer Bruce was instructed to wash Officer Waddell's truck. At the end of another shift, Officer Bruce had to clean Waddell's gutters at his home. At the end of last night's shift, Officer Waddell invited Officer Bruce to dinner with their peers, Officers Jackson and Maloof, at Shiloh's Pizzeria. At the end of the meal, Officer Waddell advised the server to give Officer Bruce the entire group's check, because he was "paying his dues." Should Officer Bruce continue to play along with these hazing rituals? What other options might he have?

What Kind of Habitat?

For the past month Officer Jenkins, a volunteer for Habitat for Humanity, has been spending shift time soliciting donations from his peers that will go toward building materials for the community's next Habitat home on Pearl Street. Almost all officers have donated a small amount of money. Some have offered to provide labor for the home's construction in lieu of a donation. Officer Thomason deeply dislikes Jenkins and has no desire to contribute his money or labor to the cause. Thomason has not submitted a grievance form to his shift supervisor, because the supervisor himself has ponied up some cash for the effort. Instead, Officer Thomason requests a meeting with the uniform patrol division's lieutenant. What should the lieutenant do?

Busting Brackets

Officers at the Canville Police Department have an annual tradition of creating a pool for the NCAA basketball tournament. Each participant in the pool contributes a few dollars and submits his or her bracket predictions. The new Chief of Police witnesses this March Madness activity and is displeased. He does not believe it is appropriate for officers to engage in such illegal gambling, especially at work. How should the new chief respond to what he has witnessed?

Put Me In, Coach!

Frontline officers in the town of Garfield Park have formed a team to play in the local co-ed adult softball league. They have been practicing and training for the long awaited games against their rivals at the local fire department. The team is concerned that one of their outfielders may have a minor injury, and they are not sure if he will be able to play. If he is unable, they will need someone else to substitute. With this in mind, they invite a particularly athletic command staff member to join their team. The command staff member is excited about the idea, but she questions whether such informal interaction will diminish her authority in the workplace. Should she play?

Community Norms Scenarios

Look the Other Way?

A local non-profit organization, specializing in providing food and clothing to domestic violence survivors and their children, is hosting a barbecue fundraiser where beer and wine will be served. This is a long-standing annual event nearing its 40th anniversary. It is understood that a few people will drink a bit more than they should before driving, but the community tends to look the other way. After all, these drunken drivers have usually donated a large amount of money to some of the area's neediest residents. Officer Lisle observes a guest staggering toward his car keys in hand. After some fumbling, the guest enters the vehicle and steers it toward the parking lot exit. What should Officer Lisle do?

What the Cluck?

While town ordinances explicitly forbid keeping any form of livestock within town limits, Ms. Judy Davis, an 80-year-old widow, has laying hens residing in her back yard. While on a routine patrol through the neighborhood, Officer Elton observes Ms. Davis feeding her chickens. What should Officer Elton do?

Ringing Ears

Lonadega is a small university town in the South. House parties are the prime form of recreation for many students residing in the community. This is especially evident on Abigail Street, comprised mainly of student rental houses and apartments. On most Thursday through Saturday nights, passersby are bombarded with loud music and chatter from partying students. The Lonadega city code specifies that after 11:00 P.M. noises at an individual residence should not exceed a volume that could be heard from 100 feet away. Officer Pabst is certain that the noise he hears as he drives through the area is in violation of the ordinance, though no residents have called to make a noise complaint. What should he do?

Mummy, Wrap It Up!

Out of recent fears regarding children's safety in the city of Camomb, local businesses have partnered with public safety agencies to offer a trick-or-treating safety zone on Halloween night. The agreement specifies that all trick-or-treating is to be concluded by 8:00 P.M. Officers Murasko and Lachey, assigned to patrol the safety zone on foot, are becoming anxious. It is almost 9:00 P.M., and some businesses are still entertaining trick-or-treaters and their parents. How should they respond?

Personal Values Scenarios

Invitation Only

Officer Pious is deeply religious and regularly attends an evangelical church in the community. One evening, she encounters a deeply troubled heroin addict in the course of a traffic stop. While the offender readily admits to possessing and using narcotics, he also asks the officer for advice on how to improve his situation in life. While Officer Pious believes spreading the gospel to the man would be inappropriate, she is considering inviting the offender to church once he has taken care of his legal issues. Would this be acceptable?

An Empty Tree

Christmas Eve shifts are the worst, and this one is only exacerbated by the fact that Ogden County deputies Miller and Weinhardt have been dispatched to the scene of "one of those calls." It seems a squirrel has found its way into a family's kitchen. The family, a woman and her two daughters, are huddled on the small deck of a shabby singlewide trailer when the officers arrive. Through the clever use of a broom, a grocery sack, and some gymnastic talents, the officers are able to capture the squirrel and secure the area. In the aftermath of the squirrel capture, both officers notice an ancient artificial Christmas tree in the living room. Whispering to the mother, they inquire whether she intends to wrap gifts for the children and place them below the tree before morning. With a profound sadness, the mother explains that she is barely making ends meet and has been unable to buy presents for this occasion. As they leave, Deputy Miller suggests to Deputy Weinhardt that they should visit the 24-hour big box store, pick up some small gifts and food for the children, and return these goods to the residence so the children will have something waiting for them in the morning. What course of action would you suggest they take?

A Ghost from the Past

Officer Wilson initiates a traffic stop. Upon approaching the vehicle, Officer Wilson is met with a pair of terrified eyes and a quivering lip, both of which belong to an 18-year-old young man who claims to be a freshman in college. In the passenger seat, Officer Wilson sees a small bag of cannabis and two joints. The driver is compliant and honest about the fact that he enjoys smoking marijuana. Something about the youth's demeanor reminds Officer Wilson of himself when he was younger. The marijuana, too, is a familiar artifact of his youth. He genuinely believes this young man is a decent enough person despite his proclivities. He certainly is more respectful than most young men with whom Officer Wilson interacts on a given shift. He is tempted to confiscate the marijuana, destroy it, and let the driver off with a warning. Should he?

Chivalry on the Job?

While on duty, Officer Sylvester stops at his favorite cafeteria for lunch. As he is eating, he overhears a man speaking disrespectfully to his female companion in the next booth over. The man chastises the woman for her choice of a burger instead of a salad, reminding her that she has put on weight since their wedding day. Despite the woman's tears and sniffles, the man continues to berate her. Officer Sylvester knows that this is not criminal behavior, but he feels compelled to intervene in this situation. What should he do?

Political Pressures Scenarios

Digging Up Some Dirt

The Elon County Commission Chairman expects a close challenge from a rival candidate. The chairman asks several deputies to use the state and national criminal databases to investigate his rival's criminal history and, if anything of interest pops up, to alert him to this information. The deputies are torn. They have no reason to run the rival through these systems, but they are aware of the considerable budgetary power the chairman wields. What should they do?

Signing Off

Bill Winesap is a long serving city council member. Officers Preeney and Sebastian catch Winesap's son, Harvey, spray painting a traffic sign. Upon arrest, Mr. Winesap arrives at the scene and begs the officers to let his son off with only a stern warning rather than a misdemeanor citation or arrest. Winesap reminds the officers that he was vocal in organizing a sufficient number of his fellow council members to vote against the mayor's proposed cuts to their pension benefits. What should Preeney and Sebastian do?

Silver Academy

A group of politically savvy senior citizens has been pressuring Chief Grayson to create a citizens' police academy so they can be more knowledgeable about how their local police department operates and become aware of potential threats to public safety in the area. Grayson is open to these requests, but he does not believe he has sufficient funds to pay for the academy. What should he do?

Other Managers Scenario

Pursuing Common Ground

Command staff members working for three separate agencies in the Tri-Cities regularly meet to discuss happenings in the area and exchange information. At an upcoming luncheon, the group plans to discuss the creation of a common pursuit policy for all agencies in the Tri-Cities area.

Deputy Chief Arnold realizes how a common pursuit policy would be helpful, especially in pursuit situations that cannot be contained in a single jurisdiction in the area. However, she fears that signing on to a common pursuit policy will limit her department's ability to make autonomous decisions or revisions in the future. How can she balance her belief in the common policy with her reservations about it?

Legal Liability Scenarios

The Naked Truth

The current strip search policy for the Shamarick County Detention Center is posted in 11-inch red letters on a white sign at the entrance to the facility. It advises all who pass the guard line that "ANYONE ENTERING THIS FACILITY IS SUBJECT TO STRIP SEARCH." In light of recent circuit court rulings from surrounding counties, the county attorney strongly suggests that the Shamarick County Sheriff revise this policy so that strip searches are only conducted on certain classes of offenders (e.g., drug offenders or those arrested for violent crimes). The Sheriff has dug his heels in and refuses to change the policy. Deputy Woody is called to the sally port to escort and book in an individual suspected of driving under the influence of alcohol. His corporal advises Deputy Woody that a strip search is mandatory for this new inmate. What should he do?

An Outside Perspective

At 3:15 A.M., Officer Huff is called to the scene of an armed robbery at an all-night convenience store. Upon arrival, Officer Huff engages an African-American suspect who begins firing at him with a Rossi Ranch Hand rifle. Officer Huff takes cover behind his patrol car and returns fire, killing the suspect. In the aftermath of this tragic event, an investigation team arrives to determine whether Officer Huff was justified in using deadly force. Simultaneously, representatives from the local NAACP chapter arrive at the scene. A representative from the NAACP asks to join the investigation team, as he suspects their determination might be biased in favor of Officer Huff before any evidence is examined. The NAACP representative threatens to sue the police department and the investigation team if he is excluded. Should he be allowed to join?

Stunning Revelations

On a rare day off, Officer Perez was lazily lounging around his home surfing Internet news sites. He saw a story about an officer in another state who had been sued after using a Stun Tech Taser on a noncompliant offender. Officer Perez felt his heart sink into his stomach, as this was one of the less than lethal weapons he regularly carries on his duty belt. He now wonders if he should avoid using his own Stun Tech even in situations where department policy would instruct him to do so in order to avoid potential legal liability. What would you tell him?

Professional Associations Scenario

Their Way or the Highway

Most officers and command staff members who work for Womack City's police department belong to a national professional association. Membership is important in many respects, as the professional association bulletin keeps these officers and administrators apprised of current trends and developments in law enforcement. The professional association has put out a model training document that it expects its members to follow. However, many officers are of the opinion that their own training documents are better focused on the realities of policing in Womack City. Should the WCPD continue to train as they have in the past, or should they use the professional association's manual?

Accreditation Bodies Scenario

Model Policies?

An agency recently secured funding from grant sources and the local legislature to pursue accreditation through a prestigious accreditation body. Both politicians and administrators believe that this accreditation will improve the agency's look and help them to avoid liability issues. However, the accreditation body mandated that the agency use a set of SOPs that are so specific that they regulate the type of undershirt that may be worn under one's bulletproof vest. Many officers and administrators have discussed the fact that these "one size fits all" policies are difficult to reconcile with the way things have traditionally been done in their agency. How can they reconcile the desire for accreditation with these concerns?

HANDS-ON TOOL D

A POST-DIAGNOSTIC GUIDE FOR STRATEGIC PLANNING

After Diagnosing with the Target Model

Once the initial Target Model diagnosis is complete, officers and command staff members have a valuable opportunity to begin deeper discussions concerning their agency's overall health and fundamental mission. To help facilitate these discussions, a progressive strategic planning tool kit is provided. This process begins with SWOT (Strengths, Weaknesses, Opportunities, and Threats) analysis. Once the SWOT analysis is complete, workers may use the discussions that follow to reconsider the larger mission or vision of their agency. From here, workers may develop short and long-term goals designed to bring the agency closer to fulfilling the created mission or vision. Finally, workers can decide upon specific, measurable, attainable, relevant, and time-bound objectives (Doran, 1981) that will help them to progress toward these goals.

SWOT

SWOT analysis is a group process that allows members of a work community to voice their opinions on the internal strengths and weaknesses an agency faces, as well as the external opportunities and threats the agency has encountered. The process usually begins with a table similar to the one provided below:

Table 13: SWOT Analysis Template

Strengths	*Weaknesses*
Opportunities	*Threats*

Each square on the SWOT table is discussed separately typically beginning with Strengths and ending with Threats. While SWOT is ultimately designed to aid later strategic planning decisions, the process of hearing and voicing opinions is valuable in and of itself. Furthermore, prior use of the Target Model can help these discussions develop more easily than if the agency is beginning from a blank slate. For instance, certain discretionary priorities (or rings) might reflect inner agency strengths and weaknesses (e.g., the level of agreement regarding the priority levels of SOPs or the agency's informal organization). Others might reflect opportunities and threats that are found outside of the agency (e.g., political pressures or community norms).

During the process of listing out each of these four categories, constructive debates may take place. For instance, one may consider an agency to have a weakness that another participant views as a strength. Through discussion between those who initially disagree, a consensus, or compromise, over these conflicting views may pave the way for a greater understanding. Once a thorough discussion has taken place and the SWOT table is complete, participants may consider a series of focusing questions, like those used by the Environmental Protection Agency.

- Where are we now? (SWOT)
- Where do we want to be? (Mission/Vision)
- How do we get there? (Goals)
- How will we measure progress? (SMART objectives)[1]

Missioning and Visioning

At this stage, participants may find it useful to consider the agency's existing mission or vision statements. Here, participants can decide if the current mission or vision statements reflect the attitudes and opinions derived from the SWOT analysis and the four focusing questions. If not, a new statement(s) may be developed.

Goal-Setting

Once a mission or vision statement for the agency has been agreed upon, participants may begin to consider possible ways in which the agency can fulfill this mission or vision over time. This can lead to the discussion of some short and long-term goals for the agency.

---

1 EPA.gov, 2013

Creating Objectives

Once a set of goals has been debated and a consensus has been reached, participants shall consider each goal separately in order to create a set of objectives that are SMART: specific, measurable, attainable, relevant, and time-bound (Doran, 1981).

The reader may notice that each stage of this strategic planning process requires more specificity and concrete detail. This is important; it links the proverbial trees to the forest and helps to reconcile the grand agendas of top-level administrators with the day-to-day work of the frontline officers. This process and the resulting plan connects those at each level of the organization and offers an opportunity for members to see the perspectives of their organizational counterparts.

OPPORTUNITY FOR REFLECTION

Why should officers, managers, and students consider aggregate studies like the one presented in this chapter in addition to single or multiple agency case studies like those presented in previous chapters?

As more research accumulates on the Target Model, scholars will ultimately decide whether or not this model can lead to generalized conclusions regarding discretionary priorities between command staff and subordinates. How will this be helpful to law enforcement agencies, students, or both?

Unlike the studies presented in previous chapters, this study does not allow for one-on-one consultation with agency officials. What does this say about the tradeoffs involved in these two very different research approaches? Which is more important: a sense of aggregate trends among hundreds of agencies or an immediate awareness of trends in one's own workplace?

This chapter focuses on county sheriffs' offices as opposed to the municipal police departments studied in previous chapters. Given that sheriffs' offices tend to have a wider variety of functions than police departments, are these two types of agencies comparable?

Chapter 7

Target Practice: Improving the Target Model and Addressing Its Limitations

Student Learning Outcomes	Practical Learning Outcomes
Students will be able to comment on the Target Model's weaknesses and how they can be improved.	Practitioners will be able to do the same. They will also be able to discuss the Target Model as a continuous organization development technique rather than a tool that is used only once.
Students will comment on ways to supplement the Target Model with academic literature.	Practitioners will comment on ways to supplement the Target Model with teambuilding, communication, and other exercises.
Students will suggest more general ways to enhance trust and communication in a classroom or workplace.	Practitioners will suggest more general ways to enhance trust and communication in the workplace or the broader field of law enforcement.

The preceding chapters showcased the versatility of the Target Model in both interview and survey research as well as in practical application. However, overall limitations of the Target Model also exist. In this chapter, I will first discuss some shortcomings of the Target Model from a practitioner's perspective, then from a scholarly perspective. I will finally explain how scholars can use the model as a starting point for future research.

Practical Limitations and Strengths of the Target Model

While the Target Model is an exciting new tool for fostering communication between public managers and their subordinates, it is not intended to work in isolation from other organization development tools and strategies. The model is a starting point designed to provide some preliminary diagnostic information to an agency rather than solving issues within the agency. In fact, the Target Model raises more questions for an agency than it answers. The attraction of the model is inherent in its ability to help managers and subordinates focus on a few areas where strong differences are observed. Thus, users of the Target Model should be able to pinpoint critical areas in discretionary decision-making that deserve more attention. The hardest work is not in making these observations but in creating an action plan to deal with them.

It is insufficient for a manager to diagnose communication differences on the topic of discretion and be unwilling to put forth the effort required to rectify these differences, or at least understand their origins. A manager who applies the Target Model should be prepared to host group discussions and training sessions regarding the findings. A manager may also find it valuable to host one-on-one meetings with subordinates to acquire more depth of perspective on their discretionary priorities. This may be more feasible in small or medium size agencies where managers have the time to host these meetings.

The Target Model is not designed to explain why differences exist, therefore, follow-up meetings and training sessions are needed. While the Target Model informs a manager of the priorities of his or her command staff and frontline officers and how these priorities differ between levels, exposing the roots or origins of these differences will require subsequent detective work. If a manager takes the first diagnostic step in applying the Target Model, he or she has a concomitant obligation to address the findings; these findings cannot be forgotten or swept under a rug. Doing so may make the manager seem lazy or unwilling to tackle flaws in his or her organization's communication system regarding the use of discretion. In many ways, the Target Model will create extra work for a manager. A committed manager (with the assistance of a willing set of employees) will welcome this opportunity. Though the work is difficult, the potential benefits of aligning many of the values of command staff members and frontline officers (or at least understanding why these values diverge) are well worth the effort. Even if these efforts do not lead to a perfect communication system, employees (and perhaps even members of the local government or populace at large) will remember that the manager was willing to put in such effort. This, in short, speaks to the manager's commitment to the agency. Such a display of commitment may have spillover benefits in terms of the level of trust the manager is capable of developing with other command staff members and frontline officers.

The development of trust can lead to even more opportunities for open discussions among employees in an agency. This is important for a couple of reasons. First, open communication can eliminate many misunderstandings and help the agency avoid internal friction and disputes. Perhaps even more importantly, this type of environment enhances employee buy-in when it comes to a manager's bigger ideas, especially those involving change. Creating an environment where employees at all levels feel comfortable in expressing their opinions and desires can even lead to a more democratic organization where employees of all ranks participate in the formulation and implementation of agency-wide decisions. At the very least, this can minimize the possibility of groupthink because it will foster critical dialogue between members of the agency. At the most, it can set the stage for strategic planning, missioning, and visioning, while additionally creating more precise goals and objectives for the agency. Focusing on the communications infrastructure surrounding the topic of discretion can set the stage for discussions of other topics and provide the manager with an opportunity to take on more of a transformational leadership role.

While most important from the internal perspective of the agency, the potential benefits of using the Target Model as a foundational step in improving the agency may also be visible to those outside the agency. This is important, as many local law enforcement managers are obligated to offer detailed explanations to city or county managers, local legislative bodies, citizens, and members of the media regarding their plans for enhancing their respective agency's operations, service capacity, and internal cohesion.

The Target Model as a Snapshot

At first sight, the Target Model can be critiqued for only providing a snapshot of a moment in time when it comes to discretionary priorities. One specific concern is that managers and frontline officers may relate their immediate priorities at a given point in time. For instance, an officer who has recently been named as a defendant in a lawsuit may be more apt to cite legal liability as a chief constraint on discretion. An officer who has just completed police academy training might be more apt to cling to an agency's standard operating procedures manual. As a final example, an officer who has had a bad run-in with the mayor or local legislative body may deem political pressures to be of heightened importance. Thus, some may argue immediate contextual factors can limit the model's utility because the model fails to capture or consider long-term trends in decision-making. This, however, is arguably one of the main strengths of the model because it forces constant replication for an agency.

Moreover, the entire premise of the Target Model is focused on assisting all employees in an agency in establishing healthy and open communication patterns. Thus, a manager may help frontline employees see how context variables shape their individual and aggregate priorities. Beyond this, a thoughtful manager may also steer officers to consider the bigger picture of agency operations and their attendant priorities. This, in turn, can foster frank and meaningful dialogue about the agency's overall vision and mission. With repeated inquiry every six months or so, the manager can get a sense of general trends among subordinates when it comes to mapping out discretionary priorities. These trends, if used appropriately, can become practically applicable beyond intra-agency strategic planning endeavors and perhaps even become the basis for budget appropriations requests each fiscal year.

In essence, the Target Model can become a starting point for a myriad of feedback loops in the agency's system. In this regard, the Target Model can drive the agency's internal and external discussions and planning processes.

GRASPING FOR OBJECTIVITY

Another potential shortcoming of the Target Model is more of a general critique on human cognition. It is difficult for managers or subordinates to step outside of themselves and see the world objectively. If each participant brings his or her own unique subject position, as described in the introductory chapter, one could argue that the responses he or she provides will always be filtered or distorted. While this is generally true, much the same can be said about most social science research. More importantly, perhaps, is that the Target Model provides an opportunity for self and group reflection to uncover these biases.

Rather than wishing individual perspectives away, scholars and managers can embrace the value of these perspectives. As with other limitations of the Target Model, the solution is to acknowledge the potential influence of one's experiences and worldviews by bringing them out in the open for critical analysis. This line of thought is already applied widely with training on various subjects (e.g., cultural diversity), bent on uncovering latent biases or misconceptions. Thus, discussions arising from use of the Target Model are likely, at a minimum, to enhance an individual officer's capacity for critical thought on the use of discretion. An optimist may claim that these discussions can help an officer or an entire agency to reconsider errant views or approaches.

This application of the Target Model may be especially useful for those on the polar opposites of the service continuum: the newest and longest-serving officers. The newest officers may need to be exposed to discussions such as these in order to shorten the length of the "John Wayne Syndrome" discussed in previous chapters. Longer-serving officers may need a fresh approach to training so that they are open to new techniques, tactics, and ways of thinking about their individual work as well as the overall work of the agency. The Target Model may be analogous to physical exercise in that it builds one's ability to move, or in this case, think more deftly. This is an important consideration given the changing nature of governance, replete with more public demands and fewer fiscal resources.

SUMMARY OF PRACTICAL LIMITATIONS AND OPPORTUNITIES

In sum, the Target Model is not intended to be a used as a magic wand to cure all ills related to the use of discretion in an agency. Instead, it is meant to be an integral piece of a larger toolkit for managers to use in analyzing their own and their subordinates' motives and values. As with any tool, the Target Model's effectiveness is largely contingent on the commitment and skill of those wielding it. While the Target Model is designed to make the work of uncovering discretionary priorities much easier than traditional approaches premised on the Doughnut Model, proper application of the Target Model still requires an appreciable amount of effort.

Managers who are simply curious about the distribution of discretionary priorities within their respective agencies may be better served by avoiding the Target Model. In many ways, the Target Model is a key that can unlock a Pandora's Box of issues that cannot be unseen. The Target Model is not helpful to those managers or subordinates who wish to perpetuate the status quo of incremental policy implementations. In most cases, the Target Model will challenge long-standing patterns of decision-making that are deeply imbedded within the organizational culture of a law enforcement department. In this respect, the Target Model can produce discomfort, frustration, and confusion.

With this in mind, the Target Model is an invitation to managers and subordinates who welcome challenges that will make them better as individual workers and yield better overall team results, in the end. For those who truly desire to improve themselves and their agencies, the Target Model can provide some of the preliminary equipment needed to produce change-oriented conversations.

THEORETICAL AND SCHOLARLY LIMITATIONS AND OPPORTUNITIES

Much of what was presented in the preceding discussion of practical limitations and opportunities is true for the Target Model as a theoretical framework. As mentioned above, the Target Model provides a window into the priorities that constrain managers and subordinates' discretionary decisions, but it falls short in offering a depth of knowledge regarding the origins of these priorities. While the Target Model is useful in fostering a broad sense of discretionary patterns, ideally it is supplemented with other methods of inquiry so that one can really appreciate these broad findings.

One potential supplemental methodology is the use of in-depth interviews with a range of organization members. Through analysis of interview exchanges, a scholar can begin to see whether organization members are offering similar rationales for similar responses. This is important as the various categories of influence leave some room for interpretation. For instance, what one person may see as a personal value may appear to another worker as an agency rule. While the strength of the Target Model is its ability to parse out discretionary influences for separate consideration, many of these categories can blend together in the real world.

More importantly, it is necessary to uncover what is contained within each of these "rings." It is insufficient to cite, for example, community norms as an influence on discretion without asking officers and managers to describe the norms that they are citing. These norms can vary from one community to another. Much the same can be said about all other categories of influence. In order to consider differences in the responses of officers and managers, scholars must first acquire a more detailed description of each response.

In addition to individual interviews, researchers might consider the use of focus groups to develop more depth of understanding. Here, the researcher should look for ways in which the group, as a whole, reaches consensus on the meaning of various discretionary influence factors. While this is important for future training endeavors related to the Target Model, it is just as important for scholarly comprehension of these categories and how they relate to one another.

In both the interview and focus group settings, a starting point, or icebreaker, may require the presentation of a realistic policing scenario. One may also consider using concise stories. Here, a researcher may find that an officer is much more willing to provide instructions to a fictional character in a story than he or she may be to openly criticize him or herself.

Broader Linkages with Existing Theory

While much of this book has focused on the nuts and bolts of applying the Target Model, the reader should not lose sight of the fact that the Target Model helps to fill a gap in the existing literature on public management. Most broadly, the Target Model provides a crucial link needed in the literature on public sector accountability. Rather than thinking about the various ways in which government agents are expected to manage expectations from various groups all at once, we typically tend to conceptualize government agents in an externally imposed, black and white phenomenon regarding them either as being accountable, or not. The Target Model builds off of previous scholarship on accountability in public administration, especially Romzek and Dubnick's (1987) four-part accountability typology. The Target Model offers more detail than this typology. It allows for the possibility of various shades of gray apparent in most discretionary choices and showcases the fact that discretionary priorities are fluid rather than static.

Thus, the Target Model is not limited to use in law enforcement agencies. Social services agencies, public works departments, parks and recreation divisions, and other local government arenas can just as easily apply it. Discretion is a universal concept in public administration, and the Target Model provides an avenue by which managers in all sorts of public agencies can arrive at a better understanding of how discretion is used in their respective offices.

Similarly, the Target Model provides a much needed mechanism by which criminal justice and public administration literatures can be reconciled. Too often, scholars in each discipline speak past one another or ignore important works in the other field. Sometimes there are discrepancies in the use of the very same word. For instance, "professionalism" is treated in criminal justice literature as being what public administration literature would call "bureaucratic accountability." How many other terms and concepts are treated differently among scholars in each field of inquiry? The Target Model can provide a common basis (and language) for the study of officer discretion. This can lend more intellectual firepower to the pursuit of understanding over officer discretion, and it can enhance other areas of overlapping research between the two disciplines. Both fields are almost certain to benefit from this change.

In short, the Target Model has tilled up some fertile research soil that future scholarship should aim to cultivate.

This book has covered quite a bit of territory, and I hope that it has opened your eyes to research questions as well as practical applications of the Target Model. In Chapter One, the concept of discretion was introduced and we shed some light on its necessity in public administration. In Chapter Two, we considered the fundamental tension between discretion and SOPs through the lenses of county sheriffs and municipal police chiefs. We learned managers want compliance with SOPs, but they also want critical thinkers working in their agencies. In essence, we discovered the need for the Target Model and its concomitant ability to help facilitate discussions about this problem.

In Part II, Chapter Three presented some real-world case studies of the Target Model's use in identifying and resolving disparate priorities between rank levels in municipal police organizations. In Chapter Four, we saw that the Target Model is also a workhorse for aggregate data analysis regarding discretionary priorities, using survey results from over 100 county sheriffs in three states.

In Part III, Chapter Five laid out the process of using the Target Model to evaluate agency communication regarding discretionary priorities, and Chapter Six offered a toolkit for managers to use in training and planning for their organizations based on the Target Model. To recap, this book has established the need for the Target Model and has presented a host of its functions in small and large research projects, face-to-face consultancy, and analysis and prediction of decision-making trends while also empowering public managers with practical skills and resources that can be leveraged to strengthen communication and planning in their respective agencies. I hope that your copy is used with dog-eared frequency, and I welcome any information scholars, practitioners, and students are willing to share about their respective experiences in using the book for research or applied practices.

OPPORTUNITY FOR REFLECTION

Given what you have read and the questions you have considered in this volume, what is the most important lesson you will take away from this book?

Why is it important to discuss the limitations of a study or set of studies?

When using the Target Model in the classroom or the squad room, how will you supplement the model to go beyond the simple diagnosis it provides?

In what ways can you enhance trust and communication in your classroom or agency? What can your command staff or professors do to enhance trust and communication?

Appendix A

Sample CALEA Written Directives[1]

CALEA Accreditation requires an agency to develop a comprehensive, well-thought-out, uniform set of written directives. This is one of the most successful methods for reaching administrative and operational goals, while also providing direction to personnel.

WRITTEN DIRECTIVES

11.4.1 Administrative reporting system

11.4.3 System to ensure periodic reports

12.2.1 Written directive system

26.1.1 Code of conduct and appearance

43.1.1 Policies for investigating vice, drug and organized crime complaints

46.1.2 An "All Hazard" Incident Command System established

52.1.5 Annual statistical summary

72.7.1 Procedure regarding detainee's rights

73.1.1 Court security function

82.1.1 Directive establishes privacy and security of records

83.2.1 Guidelines and procedures to collecting and processing evidence

Appendix B

The Target Model of Discretion

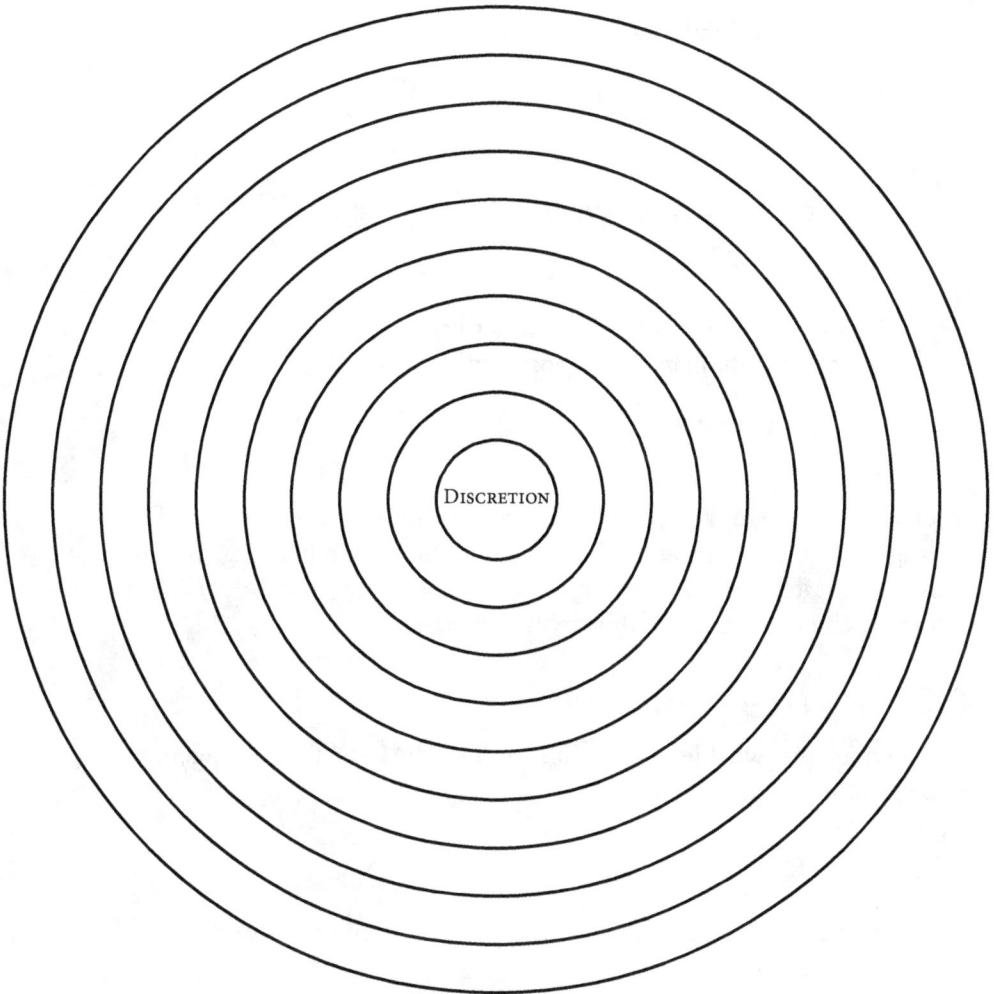

DISCRETION

TARGET SURVEY INSTRUCTION FOR PARTICIPANT

When thinking of how you use discretion as an officer, how would you rank the importance of each of the following as boundaries on discretion? That is, which do you consider most important, second most important, and so on?

1. Legal Liability (avoiding lawsuits)

2. Community Norms (fulfilling normal expectations of the community)

3. Agency Rules/SOPs (orders from supervisors or the policy manual)

4. Political Pressures (pressures from elected officials and citizens)

5. Personal Values (your own moral compass)

6. Other Managers (peers of the chief, etc.)

7. Professional Associations (IACP, NACOP, etc.)

8. Accreditation Bodies (CALEA, etc.)

9. Informal Organization Values (fitting in with the culture of the organization; getting along with coworkers)

10. Something Else

Once you have ranked each consideration, please place it in one of the rings of the target. Please only list one consideration per ring. The most important items should appear closest to the center (bull's-eye) of the target. The very center of the target represents discretion.

OPPORTUNITY FOR REFLECTION

As a manager, what led you to use the Target Model to assess agency communication?

As a frontline officer, what led you to be interested in this exercise?

What are some strengths and weaknesses of the process presented? How can this process be improved? Are there additional activities that should take place in concert with this exercise?

As a student, how can you use something like the Target Model in your classroom or student groups?

References

REFERENCES CHAPTERS ONE AND TWO

Ashworth, A., & Horder, J. (2013). *Principles of criminal law*. Oxford: Oxford University Press.

Baldi, G., & LaFrance, C. (2013). Lessons from the United States Sheriff on the Electoral Selection of Police Commissioners in England and Wales. *Policing: A Journal of Policy & Practice*, 7(2).

Briggs, J. S. (2013). *Routine justice: the intersection of race, gender and police discretion in traffic stops* (Doctoral dissertation, Kansas State University).

Caplan, G. M. (1967). The police legal advisor. *The Journal of Criminal Law, Criminology, and Police Science*, 58(3), 303-309.

Clarke, C. A., & Armstrong, K. (2012). Beyond reproach: The need for effective and responsive training. In *Police Organization and Training* (pp. 11-26). New York: Springer.

Coe, C. K., & Wiesel, D. L. (2001). Police budgeting: Winning strategies. *Public Administration Review*, 61(6), 718-727.

Crank, J., & Crank, J. P. (2010). *Understanding police culture*. New York: Routledge.

Davis, M., & Kleinig, J. (1996). Police, discretion, and professions. *Handled With Discretion: Ethical Issues in Police Decision Making*. Rowman & Littlefield.

Dworkin, R. (1977). *Taking rights seriously* (Vol. 136). Cambridge: Harvard University Press.

French, J. R., Raven, B., & Cartwright, D. (1959). The bases of social power. *Classics of organization theory*, 311-320.

Fyfe, J. J. (1996). Structuring police discretion. *Handled with discretion*, 183-205.

Gaines, L.K. & Ricks, T.A. (1978). Preface. In *Managing the Police Organization: Selected Readings*, edited by Larry K. Gaines and Truett A. Ricks. San Francisco: West Publishing Company.

Goldstein, H. (1963). Police Discretion: The Ideal versus the Real. *Public Administration Review*, 23(3), 140-148.

Gulick, L. (1937). Notes on the Theory of Organization. In *Papers on the Science of Administration*, edited by L. Gulick and L. Urwick, 1-89. New York: Institute of Public Administration.

Harmon, M. (1981). *Action Theory for Public Administration*. New York: Longman Publishing Group.

Kappeler, V. E., & Gaines, L. K. (2012). *Community policing: A contemporary perspective*. New York: Routledge.

Kleinig, J. (1996). Handling discretion with discretion. *Handled with discretion*, 1-13. New York: Rowman & Littlefield.

LaFrance, C., & Day, J. (2013). The role of experience in prioritizing adherence to SOPs in police agencies. *Public Organization Review*, 13(1), 37-48.

LaFrance, C. and S. Lee. (2010). Sheriffs' and Police Chiefs' Differential Perceptions of the Residents They Serve: An Exploration and Preliminary Rationale. *Law Enforcement Executive Forum*, 10(4): 127-38.

Law Enforcement Accreditation. (n.d.). Retrieved May 24, 2016, from http://www.calea.org/content/law-enforcement-accreditation-program

Lee, H. & Vaughn, M.S. (2010). organizational factors that contribute to police deadly force liability. *Journal of Criminal Justice*, 38(2), 193-206.

Lipsky, M. (1980). *Street-Level Bureaucracy*. New York: Russell Sage Foundation.

Lowi, T.J. (1969). *The End of Liberalism: The Second Republic of the United States*. New York: W.W. Norton & Company.

Mastrofski, S.D. (2004). Controlling Street-Level Police Discretion. *Annals of the American Academy of Political and Social Science*, 593(1), 100-18.

Maynard-Moody, S., Musheno, M. and Palumbo, D. (1990). Street-Wise Social Policy: Resolving the Dilemma of Street-Level Influence and Successful Implementation. *The Western Political Quarterly*, 43(4), 833-48.

Mayo, E. (1933). *The Human Problems of an Industrial Civilization*. New York: MacMillan.

Merton, R.K. (1940). Bureaucratic Structure and Personality. *Social Forces,* 18(4), 560-68.

Meynaud, J. (1969). *Technocracy*. New York: Free Press.

More, H.W., Wegener, W.F., Vito, G.F., and Walsh, W.F. (2006). *Organizational Behavior and Management in Law Enforcement*. Upper Saddle River, New Jersey: Pearson-Prentice Hall

Nillsson, E.K.(1972/1978). Systems Analysis Applied to Law Enforcement. In *Managing the Police Organization: Selected Readings*, edited by Larry K. Gaines and Truett A. Ricks, 325-44. San Francisco: West Publishing Company.

Nowacki, J. S. (2011). Organizational-Level Police Discretion: An Application for Police Use of Lethal Force. *Crime & Delinquency, 61*(5), 643-668.

Oberweis, T. & Musheno, M. (1999). Policing Identities: Cop Decision Making and the Constitution of Citizens. *Law & Social Inquiry,* 24(4), 897-923.

Regoeczi, W. C. and S. Kent. (2014). Race, Poverty, and the Traffic Ticket Cycle: Exploring the Situational Context of the Application of Police Discretion. *Policing: An International Journal of Police Strategies & Management,* 37(1), 190-205.

Reiner, R. (2010). *The Politics of the Police*. Oxford: Oxford University Press.

Reiser, M. (1974/1978). Some Organizational Stresses on Policemen. In *Managing the Police Organization: Selected Readings*, edited by Larry K. Gaines and Truett A. Ricks, 240-44. San Francisco: West Publishing Company.

Roethlisberger, F.J. & Dickson, W.J. (1939). *Management and the Worker*. Cambridge: Harvard University Press.

Romzek, B.S. & Dubnick, M.J. (1987). Accountability in the Public Sector: Lessons from the Challenger Tragedy. *Public Administration Review,* 47(3), 227-38.

Roussell, A. (2013). Re/Presenting the Community: Power, Race, and Division in South LA's Community Policing Program. Irvine: University of California.

Sampson, R. J. (2011). The Community. *Crime and Public Policy*, J.Q. Wilson & J. Petersilia, Eds. Oxford: Oxford University Press, 210-236.

Sims, V.H. (1988). *Small Town and Rural Police*. Springfield: Charles C. Thomas Publishers.

Skinner, B.F. (1957). *Verbal Action*. Acton: Copley Publishing Group.

Skolnick, J. H. (2011). *Justice without Trial: Law Enforcement in Democratic Society*. New York: Quid Pro Books.

Tasdoven, H. and N. Kapucu. (2013). Personal Perceptions and Organizational Factors Influencing Police Discretion: Evidence from the Turkish National Police. *International Review of Administrative Sciences*, 79(3), 523-43.

Taylor, F.W. (1911). *The Principles of Scientific Management*. New York: Harper & Brothers.

Tillyer, R. C. Klahm. (2011). Searching for Contraband: Assessing the Use of Discretion by Police Officers. *Police Quarterly*, 14(2), 166-85.

U.S. Department of Agriculture (2003). *County Urban Influence Codes*. Available on-line at: http://www.ers.usda.gov/Data/UrbanInfluenceCodes/2003/.

Walsh, W., J. Wolak, and D. Finkelhor. 2013. Sexting: When are State Prosecutors Deciding to Prosecute? The Third National Juvenile Online Victimization Study (NJOV-3). Durham, NH: Crimes Against Children Research Center.

Ward, J.D. (2002). Race, Ethnicity, and Law Enforcement Profiling: Implications for Public Policy. *Public Administration Review*, 62(6), 726-35.

Weber, M. (1946). Bureaucracy. In *From Max Weber*, edited by H. Gerth and C. Wright Mills, 196-244. New York: Oxford University Press.

Wilson, J. Q., &. Kelling, G.L. (1982). Broken Windows. *Atlantic Monthly*, 249(3): 29-38.

REFERENCES CHAPTER 3

Case 1

Barnard, C.I. (1938). *The Functions of the Executive*. Cambridge: Harvard University Press.

Blackburn, R. and B. Rosen, B. (1993). Total Quality and Human Resource Management: Lessons Learned from Baldrige Award-winning Companies. *Academy of Management Executive* 7 (3): 49-66.

Bordia, P., E. Jones, E., C. Gallos, V.J. Calla, and Nicholas DiFonzo. (2006). Management Are Aliens! Rumors and Stress During Organizational Change. *Group & Organization Management,* 31(5), 601-12.

Brandt, E. (1992). Management by 'Walking Around'. *Chemical Engineering* 99 (12): 71.

DiFonzo, N. and P. Bordia. (1998). A Tale of Two Corporations: Managing Uncertainty During Organizational Change. *Human Resource Management,* 37(3-4), 295–303.

Dworkin, R. M. (1977). *Taking rights seriously.* Cambridge: Harvard University Press.

Golembiewski, R.T. (1972). *Renewing organizations: The laboratory approach to planned change.* Itasca: F. E. Peacock Publishers.

Hirschman, A.O. (1970). *Exit, voice, and loyalty: Responses to decline in firms, organizations, and states.* Cambridge: Harvard University Press.

Houmanfar, R., & Johnson, R. (2004). Organizational implications of gossip and rumor. *Journal of Organizational Behavior Management,* 23(2-3), 117-198.

Johnson, R.R. (2010). Goal diffusion and miscommunication across rank levels. *Law Enforcement Executive Forum Journal,* 10(2), 53-63.

LaFrance, C. (2010). Professional vs. bureaucratic accountability in local law enforcement management decision-making. *Law Enforcement Executive Forum Journal,* 10(1), 147-168.

Likert, R. (1961). *New patterns of management.* New York: McGraw-Hill.

Likert, R. (1967). *The human organization: Its management and value.* New York: McGraw-Hill.

Lipsky, M. (1980). *Street-Level bureaucracy: Dilemmas of the individual in public services.* New York: Russell Sage Foundation.

Maslow, A. H. (1947). A theory of human needs. *Psychological Review,* 50(4), 370-396.

Mayo, E. (1933). *The human problems of an industrial civilization.* New York: Macmillan.

Mayo, E. (1949). *The social problems of an industrial civilization.* New York: Routledge & Kegan Paul.

McGregor, D. (1960). *The human side of enterprise.* New York: McGraw-Hill.

Merton, R. (1940). Bureaucratic structure and personality. *Social Forces, 18*(4), 560-568.

Peters, T., & Waterman, R.H. (2004). *In search of excellence: lessons from America's best-run companies.* New York: Harper Collins.

Roethlisberger, F.J., & Dickson, W.J. (1939). *Management and the worker.* Cambridge: Harvard University Press.

Serrat, O. (2009). Managing by walking around. Washington, D.C.: Asian Development Bank

Simon, H.A. (1947). *Administrative behavior.* New York: Macmillan.

Case 2

Argyris, C. (1962). *Interpersonal competence and organizational effectiveness.* Homewood, IL: Dorsey Press.

Barnard, C.F. (1938). *The functions of the executive.* Cambridge, MA: Harvard University Press.

Bordua, D.J., & Reiss, A.J. (1978). Command, control, and charisma: reflections of police bureaucracy. In L.K. Gaines & T.A. Ricks (Eds.), *Managing the police organization: Selected readings* (pp. 211-222). San Francisco: West Publishing Company.

Boyes-Watson, C. (2006). Community is not a place but a relationship: lessons for organizational development. *Public Organization Review, 5*(4), 355-374.

Bullock, K. (2010). Generating and using community intelligence: the case of neighborhood policing. *International Journal of Police Science & Management, 12*(1), 1-11.

Caplan, G.M. (1967). The police legal advisor. *Journal of Criminal Law, Criminology, and Police Science, 58*(3), 303-309.

Davis, M. (1996). Police discretion and professions. In J. Kleinig (Ed.), *Handled with discretion* (pp. 13-35). New York: Rowman & Littlefield.

Dilworth, R.L. (1996). Institutionalizing learning organizations in the public sector. *Public Productivity & Management Review, 19*(4), 407-421.

Dworkin, R. (1977). *Taking rights seriously*. Cambridge: Harvard University Press.

Frederickson, H.G. (1999). The repositioning of American public administration. *PS: Political Science & Politics, 32*(3), 701-711.

French, J.R.P., & Raven, B. (1959). Bases of social power. In D. Cartwright (Ed.), *Studies in social power* (pp. 607-623). Ann Arbor: University of Michigan Press.

Fyfe, J.J. (1996). Structuring police discretion. In J. Kleinig (Ed.), *Handled with discretion* (pp. 183-205). New York: Rowman & Littlefield.

Goldstein, H. (1963). Police discretion: The ideal versus the real. *Public Administration Review, 23*(3), 140-148.

Golembiewski, R.T. (1972). *Renewing organizations*. Ithaca: Peacock Press.

Golen, S. (1993). An analysis of communication barriers of managers in health services organizations. *Management Research News, 10*(4), 1-2.

Gulick, L. (1937). Notes on the theory of organization. In L. Gulick, & L. Urwick (Eds.), *Papers on the science of administration* (pp. 1-89). New York: Institute of Public Administration.

Henderson, D. (1985). Enlightened mentoring: a characteristic of public administration professionalism. *Public Administration Review, 45*(6), 857-863.

Hunt, D., & Michael, C. (1983). Mentorship: a career training and development tool. *Academy of Management Review, 8*(3), 475-485.

LaFrance, C. (2010). Professional vs. bureaucratic accountability in local law enforcement management decision-making. *Law Enforcement Executive Forum Journal, 10*(1), 145-165.

Lipsky, M. (1980). *Street-Level bureaucracy*. New York: Russell Sage Foundation.

Mastrofski, S. D. (2004). Controlling street-level police discretion. *Annals of the American Academy of Political and Social Science, 593*(1), 100-118.

Maynard-Moody, S., Musheno, M., & Palumbo, D. (1990). Street-wise social policy: Resolving the dilemma of street-level influence and successful implementation. *Western Political Quarterly, 43*(4), 833-848.

Maynard-Moody, S., & Musheno, M. (2003). *Cops, teachers, counselors: Stories from the front lines of public service*. Ann Arbor: The University of Michigan Press.

Mayo, E. (1933). *The human problems of an industrial civilization.* New York: Macmillan.

Meares, T. (2000). Norms, legitimacy, and law enforcement. *Oregon Law Review, 79*(2), 1-17.

Merton, R. K. (1940). Bureaucratic structure and personality. *Social Forces, 18*(4), 560-568.

Miller, J., & Davis, R. (2008). Unpacking public attitudes to the police: Contrasting perceptions of misconduct with traditional measures of satisfaction. *International Journal of Police Science & Management, 10*(1), 9-22.

More, H.W., Wegener, W.F., Vito, G.F., & Walsh, W.F. (2006). *Organizational behavior and management in law enforcement* (2nd ed.). Upper Saddle River: Pearson-Prentice

Oberweis, T., & Musheno, M. (1999). Policing identities: Cop decision making and the constitution of citizens. *Law & Social Inquiry, 24*(4), 897-923.

Parker, A., & Sarre, R. (2008). Policing young offenders: What role discretion? *International Journal of Police Science & Management, 10*(4), 474-485.

Reiser, M. (1978). Some organizational stresses on policemen. In L. K. Gaines, & T. A. Ricks (Eds.), *Managing the police organization: Selected readings* (pp. 240-244). San Francisco: West Publishing Company.

Roethlisberger, F.J., & Dickson, W.J. (1939). *Management and the worker.* Cambridge: Harvard University Press.

Romzek, B. S., & Dubnick, M. J. (1987). Accountability in the public sector: Lessons from the Challenger tragedy. *Public Administration Review, 47*(3), 227-238.

Sprafka, H., & Kranda, A. (2010). Institutionalizing mentoring in police departments. *Police Chief Magazine, 75*(1), 5-8.

Taylor, F.W. (1911). *The principles of scientific management.* New York: Harper & Brothers.

Trautman, N. (2003). Stopping political interference. *Law and Order-Wilmette then Deerfield, 51*(10), 104-111.

Case 3

Argote, L., McEvily B., & Reagans, R. (2003). Managing knowledge in organizations: An integrative framework and review of emerging themes. *Management Science 49*(4), 571-582.

Argyris, C. (1962). *Interpersonal competence and organizational effectiveness.* Homewood: Dorsey Press.

Barnard, C.F. (1938). *The functions of the executive.* Cambridge: Harvard University Press.

Denhardt, J., & Denhardt, R. (2003). *The new public service: Serving, not steering.* Armonk: M.E. Sharpe.

Dworkin, R. (1977). *Taking rights seriously.* Cambridge: Harvard University Press.

Fyfe, J.J. (1996). Structuring police discretion. In J. Kleinig (Ed.), *Handled with discretion* (pp.183-205). New York: Rowman & Littlefield.

Gaines, L.K. (1978). Overview of organizational theory and its relation to police administration. In L.K. Gaines & T.A. Ricks (Eds.), *Managing the police organization: Selected readings* (pp. 151-178). San Francisco: West Publishing Company.

Golembiewski, R.T. (1972). *Renewing organizations.* Ithaca: Peacock Press

LaFrance, C. (2010a). Professional vs. Bureaucratic Accountability in Local Law Enforcement Management Decision-making. *Law Enforcement Executive Forum Journal, 10*(1), 145-165.

LaFrance, C. (2010b). Back to the Firing Range: An Exploratory Test of the Target Model of Discretion. *Law Enforcement Executive Forum, 10*(4), 167-174.

Mayo, E. (1933). *The Human Problems of an Industrial Civilization.* New York: MacMillan.

Maynard-Moody, S., Musheno, M., & Palumbo, D. (1990). Street-Wise social policy: Resolving the dilemma of street-level influence and successful implementation. *The Western Political Quarterly, 43*(4), 833-848

Oberweis, T., & Musheno, M. (1999). Policing identities: Cop decision making and the constitution of citizens. *Law & Social Inquiry, 24*(4), 897-923.

Reiser, M. (1974/1978). Some organizational stresses on policemen. In L.K. Gaines & T.A. Ricks (Eds.), *Managing the police organization: Selected readings* (pp. 240-244). San Francisco: West Publishing Company.

Roethlisberger, F.J. & Dickson, W.J. (1939). *Management and the worker.* Cambridge: Harvard University Press.

Tyler, T.R., & Huo, Y.J. (2002). *Trust in the law: Encouraging public cooperation with the police and courts.* New York: Russell Sage Foundation.

REFERENCES CHAPTER 4

Falcone, D.N. & Wells, L.E. (1995). The county sheriff as a distinctive policing modality. *American Journal of Police, 14*(3), 123-149.

Janis, I. (1982). *Groupthink.* New York: Houghton Mifflin Company.

Kemelgor, B.H. (1982). Job satisfaction as mediated by the value congruity of supervisors and their subordinates. *Journal of Occupational Behavior, 3*(2). Retrieved from http://www.jstor.org/stable/3000081

LaFrance, C. (2010). Professional vs Bureaucratic Accountability in Local Law Enforcement Management Decision-making. *Law Enforcement Executive Forum Journal, 10*(*1*), 145-165.

LaFrance, C. & Placide, M. (2010a). Sheriffs' and police chiefs' leadership and management decisions in the local law enforcement budgetary process: An exploration. *International Journal of Police Science and Management, 12*(2), 238-255.

LaFrance, C. and Placide, M. (2010b). A quantitative analysis of accountability indicators in sheriffs' offices and municipal police departments. *Law Enforcement Executive Forum Journal,* 10(2), 107-120.

Lewis-Beck, M. (1980). *Applied regression: An introduction.* Sage publications.

McKnight, D.H., Cummings, L.L., & Chervany, N.L. (1998). Initial trust formation in new organizational relationships. *The Academy of Management Review, 23*(3), 473-490. Retrieved from http://www.jstor.org/stable/259290

Organ, D.W. (1988). *Organizational citizenship behavior: The good soldier syndrome.* Lexington: Lexington Books.

Suchman, M.C. (1995). Managing legitimacy: Strategic and institutional approaches. *The Academy of Management Review, 20*(3), 571-610. Retrieved from http://www.jstor.org/stable/258788

Veiga, J.F. (1988). Face your problem subordinates now! *The Academy of Management Executive, 2*(2), 145-152. Retrieved from http://www.jstor.org/stable/4164816

Whetten, D.A. (1978). Coping with incompatible expectations: An integrated view of role conflict. *Administrative Science Quarterly, 23*(2), 254-271. Retrieved from http://www.jstor.org/stable/2392564

REFERENCES CHAPTER 5

LaFrance, C. (2010). Back to the firing range: An exploratory test of the target model of discretion. *Law Enforcement Executive Forum, 10*(4), 167-174.

Thompson, J. (1967). *Organizations in action: Social science bases of administrative theory*. New Brunswick: Transaction.

REFERENCES CHAPTER 6

Doran, G.T. (1981). There's a S.M.A.R.T. way to write management's goals and objectives. *Management Review, 70* (11), 35-36.

US EPA. (n.d.). Retrieved May 24, 2016, from http://www2.epa.gov/aboutepa/epa-information-resources-management-strategic-plan

REFERENCE CHAPTER 7

Romzek, B.S., & Dubnick, M.J. (1987). Accountability in the public sector: Lessons from the Challenger tragedy. *Public Administration Review, 47*(3), 227-238.

www.ingramcontent.com/pod-product-compliance
Lightning Source LLC
Chambersburg PA
CBHW061751270326
41928CB00011B/2463